ROBBIE & GEORGE

By Rob Morin

Illustrations by Larry Daley

Robbie & George

Copyright 2022 by Rob Morin

Illustrations by Larry Daley

All rights reserved. No part of this book may be reproduced without permission of the author.

Published by Piscataqua Press

32 Daniel St., Portsmouth, NH 03801

info@piscataquapress.com

ISBN: 9781958669044

Printed in the United States of America

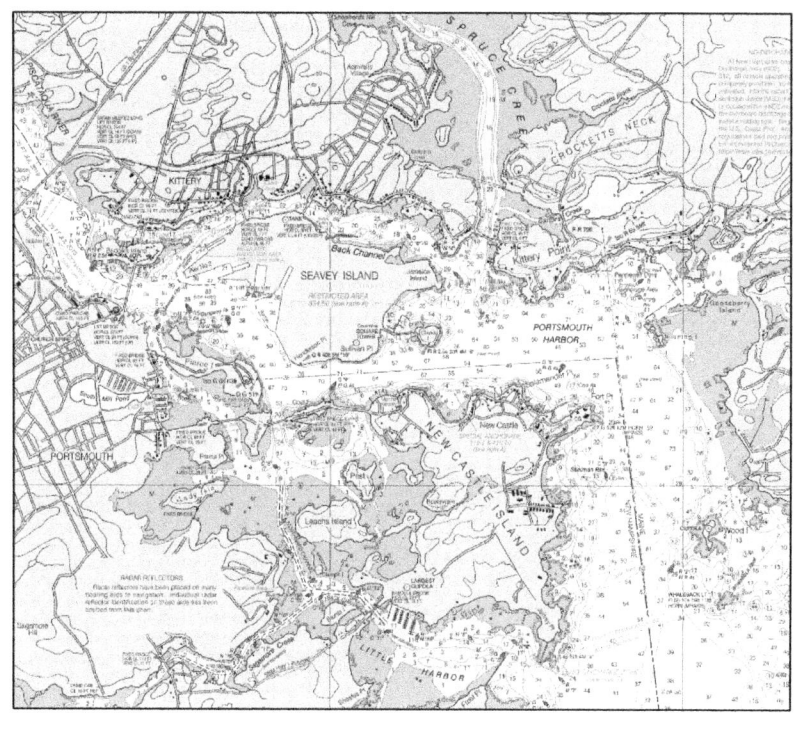

Portsmouth Harbor and Spruce Creek

This story is written in memory of and as a tribute to my terrific Mother and Father, Betsy and Bob Morin and to the wonderful Rose Labrie…three people who changed my life forever.

A Most Unusual Friendship

In the summer of 1974, in the busy seaport of Kittery, Maine, lived one most unusual seagull alongside the thousands of ordinary gulls that swooped and squabbled along the shoreline.

This seagull stood out from all the other gulls, not because it was fat or skinny, big or small, but because it was always alone, as if it had no friends nearby, even on a small island crowded with lots of other seagulls.

It was a handsome bird with distinct colorings, and it kept itself very clean and tidy. The white feathers on its body were bright white and its big wing feathers were a shiny gray with dark black tips. Its beak was different too: large, orange, and glossy. When it flew, the undersides of its wings were bright white except for the crisp black edges. It flew with grace and confidence. It usually landed on its favorite rock, near Seavey Island, far away from all the other gulls. Seagulls are smart and have keen eyesight, and this one didn't miss a trick. It would stand proud on its rock in the warm sun and watch the world go by.

There were many other kinds of birds there, too. There were terns, ducks, and double-crested cormorants. There were blue jays, red cardinals, doves, sparrows, and even little finches that would stop on the rock momentarily and visit with the seagull. The seagull welcomed them, because sometimes he got along better with birds of a different kind than he did with birds of his own kind. Sometimes, when other seagulls came by, maybe two or three at a time, they would swoop down to pick on him and try to chase it off its rock so they could land there. Sometimes, they would even try to steal his food.

A small river, called the Back Channel, ran between the Kittery dock and Seavey Island. There were several boats moored in the Back Channel, both motorboats and sailboats. Robbie, a nine-year-old boy, lived on one of those boats with his parents.

Sometimes, Robbie felt just like that seagull. Sometimes kids at school picked on him, too, and he didn't like it either. One time, three kids backed him into a corner on the playground and forced him to hand over his lunch money: twenty-five cents! He never told his parents about it, but that year he couldn't wait for the school year to end and for his family's summer vacation to begin.

Robbie and his parents, Mr. and Mrs. Morin, spent their winters in a house, but in the summer they moved

An Unusual Friendship

aboard their 42-foot motorboat, named *My Fair Lady*. They tied *My Fair Lady* to a floating dock at Dion's Yacht Yard in the Back Channel, just across the channel from the big rock where the unusual seagull often stood.

Even though it meant leaving home behind, Robbie absolutely loved living on the boat. *My Fair Lady* had a galley (kitchen), two small staterooms (bedrooms) and a head (bathroom). There was so much to do and see. Each morning, Robbie awoke to the sound of waves lapping against the hull. At night, snug in his sleeping bag on his bunk, he drifted off to sleep to the sound of the foghorn from Whaleback Lighthouse. Every day, he watched the red tugboats carefully guide passing ships in and out of the narrow harbor entrance. Robbie loved those tugboats and dreamed that one day he could be a tugboat captain. There were real submarines being built at the nearby Portsmouth Naval Shipyard, too. Robbie was very curious about the submarines and how they might be used in battles.

And best of all, there was fishing in *Dr. Dolittle*, their 13-foot-long Boston Whaler, known to be safe and unsinkable. *Dr. Dolittle* was like a family car but on the water. They could go to any place that was accessible by water, like the grocery store, restaurants, even the post office! They also used *Dr. Dolittle* to visit nearby islands, the yacht club, and other boaters in the harbor. *Dr. Dolittle* was usually just called *Dolittle*, for short.

Robbie's parents loved him, and they taught him how

to handle the risks of living on a boat. He learned early on how to swim. He learned how to move safely between the floating docks and the boats, and how to be careful and agile while aboard *My Fair Lady*.

"One hand for you, one hand for the boat!" his mother often said.

One day, while eating their lunch, Robbie's father rolled out a navigational chart of the harbor, much like a map one would use for driving a car. He taught Robbie the basics of reading the chart, what the symbols meant, and where their location was on the chart. They went up to the bridge (the upper deck) of *My Fair Lady* together, and his father pointed to the different markers in the channel. He showed Robbie exactly where those markers were located on the chart and where *My Fair Lady* was docked in relation to those markers.

After lunch, his mom taught him to clean up the galley of *My Fair Lady* and then the two of them got onboard *Dolittle*. His Mom taught Robbie the layout of the boat: the bow (the front), the stern (the back), port (left) and starboard (right). She taught him when it was safe to stand up in *Dolittle*, when to sit down, and when to hold on to the ropes and railings. Robbie learned about the tides and currents (which could be quite drastic at times), and how much or how little speed it takes to move through the water in different conditions. Mrs. Morin showed Robbie how to start the engine by pulling the starter cord, how to use the throttle to speed up or slow down, the gear shift to go forward and reverse and how to properly steer the boat. He also learned how to tie knots and secure *Dolittle* to the cleats on the dock.

When it was time to see how much Robbie had learned, his mother untied the lines and off they went together for a ride in *Dolittle* with Robbie at the helm (steering wheel) for the first time. He was in charge and held his head high! When they got back to the dock from their ride around the harbor, Robbie tied the boat to the dock, shut off the engine and his mother got out of the boat saying, "Well done!"

Then his father got into the boat. "Hey! What about me?" he said. "I want to go for a ride too!"

Robbie happily pulled the starter cord and untied the lines again. He drove the whole time he was with his father. Mr. Morin taught Robbie the meaning of the floating markers called *Red Nuns* and *Green Cans*, the same ones he had shown him on the chart. Those mark the channel, much the same way the yellow and white lines on a road mark the lanes where it's safe to drive a car.

"Keep in mind, it's Red, right, returning!" his dad taught Robbie. "All boats always keep the red markers on the right side of the boat when returning from sea and it's the opposite going out to sea where green markers would be on the right." Outside of those markers are *hazards* like rocks and sandbars, and in Maine, the dangerous rocks are more like boulders! Hitting a rock could do real

Robbie & George

damage to a boat or, as his father said, with a smirk on his face, "One rock could ruin your whole day!"

Using *Dolittle* was a privilege. His parents gave him important ground rules to follow, and they made very certain that he knew them. The first rule was that he was to stay within sight, which meant for him to take the boat only within certain boundaries around the little cove and in the Back Channel. He was not to go past the *Green Can Number 3* to the south or beyond the *Green Can Number 7* to the north. Second was that he had to always wear a life jacket. Third was that he must make sure he had enough gas in the gas tank before he went out in the boat. Finally, he had to keep *Dolittle* washed and clean, particularly when he came back from fishing. Once they were sure he understood these simple rules, and after a few more test rides together, his parents allowed Robbie to take *Dolittle* out exploring and fishing on his own. That way, Robbie could be safe yet independent.

Early one morning, Mr. and Mrs. Morin were chatting with another couple about boring adult stuff and Robbie was feeling a bit lonesome. A great time to go fishing! he thought. So, he wrapped a chocolate doughnut in a napkin, stuffed it in his jacket pocket, and grabbed a carton of milk. He gathered his fishing gear, put on his life jacket, and checked the gas tank to make sure there was enough gas. With a pull of the cord, he started *Dolittle's* outboard motor and chugged away from the dock.

An Unusual Friendship

Once he was out in the cove, but still within sight of his parents, he lowered the anchor and waited for it to dig into the soft, muddy bottom. Looking up, he noticed that unusual seagull sitting on the rock across the harbor again. Robbie looked at the seagull and wondered why it was all alone. Did it, too, feel lonesome with no friends? He wondered if seagulls had brothers and sisters. He wondered if its parents were visiting with all the other seagulls nearby, much like his parents were chatting with their friends just behind him aboard *My Fair Lady*.

As he sat there fishing, he had a strange feeling that the seagull was watching *him*, too. It was as if they were talking to each other without using words. But that's impossible, thought Robbie, right?

Just then, as if the seagull was reading Robbie's mind, it stood up, spread its wings, and flew away. It soared high in the air and made two big, wide circles around the harbor and around *Dolittle* before landing on the deck of a sailboat named *Sunday's Child*, just a short distance from Robbie. The seagull quickly shook its body, tilted its head from side to side, wiggled its wings as if to put them back in place, and settled in. Then it stood as still as could be on the stern of the sailboat, watching Robbie fish. *Sunday's Child* swung slowly from side to side on its mooring, but the seagull never changed position, nor did it lose sight of him.

Robbie & George

An Unusual Friendship

It was a beautiful, calm Saturday morning. Robbie decided to head back to shore and continue fishing from the dock. The tide in that area was fourteen feet, meaning at high tide the harbor was full of water that had come in from the ocean, making the water in the harbor deeper, meaning there would be more fish. At low tide, the water in the harbor would go back out to sea and the level of the harbor would drop fourteen feet, making it shallow enough to sometimes see the bottom when the conditions were just right. The tides are controlled by the moon and the sun and there are two high tides and two low tides every day. The *current* is the speed at which the water flows. When the tide is exactly at high or low, the water, incredibly, stands still and doesn't move at all until it either turns to come in or go out, and that is called slack tide.

Mr. and Mrs. Ellis rowed past Robbie in their dinghy during slack tide on their way out to their boat, *Sunday's Child*. As Robbie was eating his doughnut and drinking his milk, they called across, "Good Morning, Robbie!"

Robbie called back, "Good Morning!" as they passed.

"Catching anything?" Mr. Ellis asked.

"Nope, not yet." Robbie said.

Mr. Ellis stopped rowing and drifted along. He looked all around at the shoreline, looked up at the sky, started rowing again and said, "Hang in there Robbie, tides about high, don't give up, never give up," and he continued to row.

Robbie & George

Just as they were about to step from their little rowboat and onto their sailboat, Robbie shouted, "Mr. and Mrs. Ellis, there's a seagull on your boat!"

Most people do not like seagulls because they are known to be dirty. They poop on the boats, so people often shoo them away. Sometimes boaters will tie up a long line from the bow to the stern of their boats, with little colored flags attached to the line. The flapping of the flags in the breeze is supposed to scare the seagulls away. Mr. and Mrs. Ellis had no such contraption on their boat. They called back to Robbie, "It's okay, it's just George! Come on over and say hi to him."

Robbie wound his fishing line around a little wooden block, sometimes called a yoyo, hopped into *Dolittle*, and paddled over to *Sunday's Child*, tying the boat up alongside. Climbing aboard, he sat with the Ellises in the cockpit while the seagull stood on the side deck. The bird tilted his head from one side to the other, peering at the newcomer with curiosity.

Mr. Ellis said, "It's okay, George, come on in. This is Robbie."

It took time, but George stepped slowly and cautiously across the deck of the boat, around the folded yellow sail cover, and hopped into the cockpit.

George stood next to Robbie, looking at him.

Robbie felt a thrill being so close to this beautiful wild bird, and George felt very bold coming so close to a new person.

An Unusual Friendship

Mr. Ellis said to Mrs. Ellis, "Jeannie, how about getting a half a piece of bread for George?"

Robbie burst out laughing, watching them feed the bread to George. Then they gave Robbie some bread so he could feed George, too. They were all laughing and having lots of fun.

Robbie was surprised and disappointed when Mr. Ellis said, "Well, Robbie, we have to get going. We are starting out soon on a long cruise up the coast of Maine towards Bar Harbor. We'll be away sailing all summer, so we have to finish getting our supplies and food aboard and packed away."

"Okay," said Robbie with a sigh.

"Jeannie," Mr. Ellis asked his wife, "do we have flashlight batteries on the list?"

"Check!" she said.

"And how about extra gooseberry jam? I'm a much better navigator if I have gooseberry jam on my toast."

"Of course!" she said, holding up a jar. Mrs. Ellis stood up to check her lists, and at her movement, George stepped carefully back out onto the deck.

As he returned to *Dolittle*, Robbie felt that lonely feeling come over him again like a shadow. He liked the Ellises because they were such nice people, and it saddened him that they would soon sail away for the summer. He said goodbye and wished them safe sailing. He untied his bow line and drifted a short distance back and slowly, he slid his anchor and line over the side of

Dolittle and waited for it to catch hold. He put a fresh sea worm on the hook, lowered it over the side and tied off the fishing line. He rinsed his hands in the salt water and when they no longer smelled like sea worms, he settled down to eat the rest of his breakfast and think.

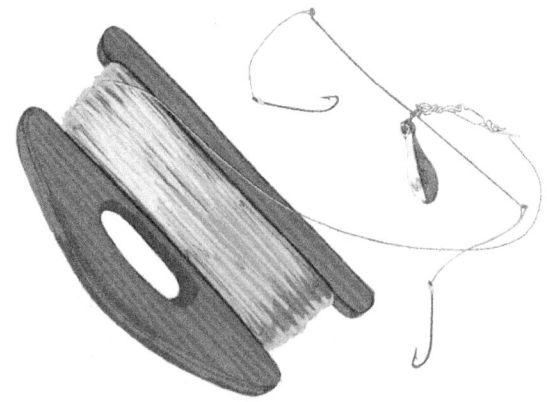

An Unusual Friendship

Fishing was really good for thinking because it's peaceful and quiet, with long periods of waiting. Robbie was fishing with a hand line, which is different from using a fishing pole. He used a hand line to catch fish that were at the bottom of the sea and a fishing pole to catch the ones near the surface of the sea. After baiting a hook on a hand line, he would slowly slide the line over the side of the boat to let it sink down to the bottom. Here's the fisherman's secret, though: when the sinker hits the bottom, he needs to pull the line up six to twelve inches to get the sinker off the bottom, but not too much. It needs to be just enough so that the worm and hook stay on the bottom where the fish are feeding, but the sinker, a little lead weight that keeps the line from drifting, is above the mud. That way when you hold the line in your hand, you can feel the fish nibbling at the worm and tugging on the line. If the sinker is sitting in the mud on the bottom, you won't feel anything. Sometimes Robbie caught crabs and lobsters that way, too. When that happened, the trick was to haul them in as fast as possible, because as soon as crabs and lobsters detect the surface sunlight, they let go of the worm and the line and slowly sink back down to the bottom. Sometimes, you can catch two fish at once because there are two hooks, and when that happens, it's called a "Double Header!"

Robbie sat in *Dolittle*, thinking about everything and thinking about nothing at the same time. While waiting for the tug on his fishing line, Robbie could hear Mr. and

Robbie & George

Mrs. Ellis talking because they were so close, and the air was so still, you could hear a pin drop

He watched as they raised their main sail to keep the boat steady. Mrs. Ellis cast away their mooring line and Mr. Ellis turned the tiller hard to port, waiting for the breeze to pick up and for the sail to fill with wind. As they were drifting away with the outgoing tide and waiting for wind, Mr. Ellis looked at George and said, "George, you go on now, you can't come with us. You go with Robbie and you keep an eye on him, you hear?"

Then Mr. Ellis looked over at Robbie sitting in *Dolittle* and called out, "Robbie, you take care of George too, okay?"

Robbie waved goodbye and said, "I promise!"

Within seconds, George took flight off the deck of the sailboat. The wind picked up, and as *Sunday's Child* gained speed George soared way up into the air and followed the Ellises out of the harbor. He went so far away that Robbie lost sight of him for minutes at a time. The sinking sense of loneliness returned to Robbie, a feeling that he would likely never see George again. Way out in the distance, he saw George making three big, wide circles around *Sunday's Child* as if to salute the Ellises and say goodbye to them. Then George flew off out of sight of both Robbie and *Sunday's Child*. Robbie slumped back down in the boat, feeling blue.

"I am really going to miss the Ellises, and now George seems to be flying away, too," Robbie said aloud with a

An Unusual Friendship

sigh as he watched *Sunday's Child* get smaller and smaller as it sailed off toward the horizon. He tugged on his line to see if he had a fish, but there was nothing. "And now I betcha a flounder stole my bait!"

He pulled the line in and the worm was gone. "That's what I get for not paying attention." Despite feeling discouraged, Robbie pulled another sea worm from his bait can, slipped it onto his hook, and dropped the line over the side again with a little plop, mumbling, "Don't give up, never give up."

He leaned over the side to rinse his hands again. Then he leaned way over, cupped his hands together, and splashed some salt water on his face. He loved doing that. It felt refreshing, like swimming at the beach, and it tasted very salty. Each drop that fell off his nose and chin hit the calm water below and created little ripples that went away from the boat.

Staring into the water, Robbie could perfectly see the reflection of his own face, and the blue sky, sun, and clouds above him.

It amazed him that he could look down into the water and see the sky above, but he couldn't look up into the sky and see the water. Just then, something else appeared in the reflection of the water that made Robbie blink his eyes in disbelief.

An Unusual Friendship

Looking into the water, he could see a seagull flying above *Dolittle*. Robbie stood up quickly and wiped his face dry on his sleeve. He raised his right hand up to shade the sun from his eyes so he could scan the sky above and at first, he didn't see anything. He looked back down into the water and up again and soon he spotted the seagull making wide circles around the harbor, surveying the whole situation. A warm feeling suddenly came over Robbie. With impressive speed and precision, the bird dove down from high in the sky, came to a screeching halt and landed gracefully on its feet on the bow of *Dolittle*. It was George! George quickly shook his body, tilted his head from side to side, wiggled his wings as if to put them back in place and perched there looking at Robbie as if to say: "All right, what's next?"

Eyes wide open, Robbie stood frozen, staring at George, trying not to scare him away. Before today, he had never been so close to a seagull and now, for the second time in less than an hour, here was George, standing right there on *Dolittle* four feet away from him, and not moving a muscle. As the two of them studied each other, Robbie saw and heard his line go out quickly and the Yoyo skid across the bottom of the boat smacking into the side. He stepped on it before it flew out of the boat, picked it up and felt a big tug on the other end. He gave it a quick yank to set the hook so the fish, if there was one, could not get away. Robbie pulled and pulled, hauling the line in as the fish fought on the other end.

"HOLY COW GEORGE! Look at that fish!" he cried as it came to the surface. "IT'S A WHOPPER!"

Robbie hauled it up over the side of *Dolittle*, and it landed on the floor of the boat, flopping around like crazy. It was indeed a fish, and George looked at it with great interest.

An Unusual Friendship

The seagull cocked his head to one side, then the other, and back again. He quickly paced around the edge of the boat from the bow towards the stern, clearly excited about getting a closer look at the fish. He stretched his neck out and lowered his head towards the fish to get a better view.

It amazed Robbie that George could balance on such a narrow edge, using only slight adjustments of his wings and body weight to steady himself. As George peered at the fish, he looked super puzzled, almost like he had never seen a fish before. It smelled like a fish and flopped around in the boat like a fish, but it sure didn't look like one! It was a flat fish called a flounder (or sole), the size of an extra-large dinner platter, with two eyes close together on one side of its head but no eyes on the other side.

Weird, George thought!

The flounder was dark brown on one side and a beautiful glossy white on the other. Robbie realized why George was so confused. George must have only ever seen fish that swim near the surface of the sea where a seagull can snatch them. He had probably never seen a fish that swims on the bottom of the sea.

"Don't worry," Robbie assured George, "flounders are still good eating, especially the way Mom cooks them, with breadcrumbs, and lemon squeezed on top!"

Once he landed that fish, big enough for his family's dinner, Robbie pulled up the anchor, started the engine, and slowly puttered back to the dock. His mother was standing waiting for him. She had her apron on and was ready to cook dinner.

"My!" she said. "What do we have here, a trophy fish? Good for you! And it looks like you have a new friend, too."

An Unusual Friendship

"Yeah! You should have seen me pulling it in, Mom, it was a real fighter!" Robbie said with excitement. "And that's George. He's really smart. We were fishing together, and he's never seen a flounder before!"

Robbie tied the lines to the cleat, securing *Dolittle* to the dock, and swung his bucket ashore. He took off his life jacket, knelt on the dock next to the hose, and filleted the fish for dinner. The previous summer, his mother had taught him how to scrape off the scales on the brown side of the fish and carefully cut the tasty meat away from the bones with a sharp knife called a filet knife, made for just that purpose. He threw the scraps of fish to George. As George got more comfortable and saw that Robbie and his mom weren't going to hurt him, or shoo him away like most people would, he got closer and closer. Before long, George was standing right next to Robbie, happily cleaning up the scraps being tossed to him, sometimes catching them in midair and gobbling them down as Robbie and his mother watched along, laughing.

"You're such a good provider, son, I think I'll quit my job," joked Robbie's father at the dinner table as he tucked into the succulent, pan-fried flounder and the coleslaw that Robbie's mother had made. "Look at the size of that filet!" Robbie was proud of the recognition, but he knew he was a long way from taking his dad's place.

His mother said with a wink, "I think you've earned a slice of strawberry rhubarb pie – if you'd like some."

"Oh yes, Ma'am, with ice cream please!"

Robbie & George

After helping his mother clean up the galley, he went above decks and whispered ever so quietly, "Good night, George," unsure of where he was. He got into his pajamas and climbed into his sleeping bag in his bunk. He was lulled asleep by the sound of Whaleback Lighthouse's foghorn; Whhoooommp, Whhoommp, Whhoooommmp. It was deep and spooky, yet somehow comforting, too.

Whaleback Lighthouse is one of many lighthouses standing along the rocky seacoast of Maine. When the sun goes down and it starts to get dark, lighthouses come alive and flash a unique light signal every few seconds so that mariners can find the entrance of a safe harbor during the night. Every lighthouse flashes a different signal. When the weather is foggy and ships cannot see the light, lighthouses are also equipped with foghorns that sound a unique horn signal as well. Mariners on ships in the thick fog can hear the unique sound of the lighthouse's horn so they can determine their location along the coast. It is possible, in thick fog, that a mariner could hear the foghorn and still never see the light on the lighthouse even as they pass right by it. Whaleback Lighthouse marked the dangerous harbor entrance of the Piscataqua [pis-CAT-ah-kwah] River. There are boulders and rocks everywhere and a mariner must always be prudent. Robbie loved the foghorn's deep tone. It lulled him to sleep, reminding him that he, too, was a mariner and someday he would be listening to and looking for that same lighthouse at the mouth of the river. For now, he was safe in his bunk. He dreamt about George and wondered where George was sleeping, and if seagulls even slept. He wondered if they dreamt and if they did dream, what did they dream about?

Breaking the Rules

When Robbie woke up the next morning, he rushed to the windows of the upper cabin and looked out to see if he could find his new friend, George. It was so foggy, cool, and damp that he couldn't see much at all. If his mom were awake, she'd call it a "dumb day," a good day to stay in bed. Whaleback Lighthouse was still sounding its horn and most of the boats, even the work boats, stayed put, waiting for the fog to lift. It was eerily quiet, all except for the unmistakable rumble of an engine running way off in the distance, which could only be old Gus Alley's lobster boat, named the *Leonard W.*, the fastest (and loudest) lobster boat in the world.

Robbie could just barely see across the harbor, but George was not on his rock nor anywhere in sight. He listened carefully for stirrings from the other cabin, but there were none, so he knew his parents were still asleep. In his pajamas and bare feet, he tiptoed outside onto the wet deck and looked all around, but there was no George.

Slowly and ever so quietly, he stepped off *My Fair Lady* and onto the creaky old wet dock, checking the pilings, the planks, and the damp, foggy sky above. George was nowhere to be found.

Although the bottoms of his pajamas were already soaking wet from the rainwater on the docks, Robbie marched past the dinghy dock and up the ramp and into the boat yard. He hopped over the greasy cables of the marine railway that was used to haul boats out of the water. As he passed the old Pepsi machine he saw a row of seagulls, but none of them were George. In the dirt parking lot where boats were normally stored in the wintertime, there were several more gulls, but none of them were George.

"George, George!" he whispered loudly. "Where are you? Have any of you seen George?" he asked the other gulls, but none of them answered. He shrugged and made a circuit around the boat yard, peering around cars, trucks, and boats that were out of the water for repairs. He walked up the small rise, around the paint shed, and back down through the crushed stone parking lot.

"Ouch!" he said under his breath, picking a sharp stone out from between his toes. Shivering from the damp cold, he returned to *My Fair Lady*, thinking he may as well climb back into his warm bunk as it was still very early. Besides, he could sneak a small doughnut out of the box in the galley since it was right on the way!

Before getting aboard *My Fair Lady*, while holding onto

the railing, he dipped his left foot into the water, swishing it around to wash off the sand and dirt, then his right foot. When he glanced up, there was George! He had been sleeping on the dock next to the step the whole night, right outside the porthole next to Robbie's bunk. "Wow, I didn't even see you, George!" Robbie whispered.

Robbie changed his plan (except for the doughnut part). Instead of going back to bed, he whispered to George, "Get ready to leave. We're going on an adventure!"

Quietly, Robbie slipped back aboard *My Fair Lady* and tiptoed below to change into his clothes. He got his jacket and took a quarter out of his allowance money. In the galley, he grabbed a chocolate doughnut for himself and a plain one for George, wrapped them in a paper napkin, and stashed them in his pocket. He looked in the fridge and took a carton of milk to go with the doughnut and managed to get back off the boat without waking his parents.

Breaking the Rules

Slowly and cautiously, the boy and the bird boarded *Dolittle* without making a sound or a ripple in the water. Robbie put on his life jacket, checked the fuel, and untied the lines and they paddled away in the fog. Once they were far enough away to start the motor without waking anyone up, Robbie pulled on the starter cord and the engine came to life. They slowly motored away as the fog began to lift. When it was clear enough for them to continue their mission, Robbie sped up by pushing the throttle forward. They sped north through the Back Channel, past the *Green Can Number 5* and past the forbidden *Green Can Number 7*.

The tide was slack, so the water was very calm. Robbie saw that they could make a move to cross the river and now was the perfect time. They went under the two Navy Yard bridges, past the *Leonard W.*, and across the Piscataqua River which separates Maine from New Hampshire and leads to the Atlantic Ocean. Robbie was not supposed to be crossing it and he knew it. The Piscataqua is the third fastest tidal river in North America, and his parents said the tides, currents, and sometimes waves from the other boats make it very dangerous. If they found out what a risk he was taking, Robbie would be in big trouble. George thought the same. But Robbie really wanted to go fishing; the best worms were from Brewster's Bait Shack across the river in Portsmouth. He felt confident in his ability to pilot *Dolittle*, and didn't think it was really that dangerous.

Robbie & George

They made it to Brewster's and tied the bow line onto the cleat of the rickety floating dock. George stayed and watched over *Dolittle* as Robbie walked up the crooked ramp, wiping the salty dew from his face with his sleeve.

Breaking the Rules

Inside the shack, he announced to crusty old Mr. Brewster, "I'd like a dozen sea worms, Sir!"

The shack was built out above the water on stilts. Mr. Brewster sat in a worn, sagging chair drinking coffee and listening to the news. The AM radio had an upside-down coat hanger for an antenna, and the man wore stained, grubby fisherman's work trousers and a plaid shirt. He looked like he had been sitting there forever, though it was only seven o'clock in the morning. Mr. Brewster squinted at Robbie through his thick, dirty glasses. Robbie could tell from that look that Mr. Brewster knew that Robbie knew that his parents *didn't* know that he was there. If they *did* know, Mr. Brewster knew that Robbie knew he would be in serious trouble.

Saying nothing, the old man got up out of his chair and limped over the splintery floorboards toward the old-fashioned cash register and the telephone on the counter. He plunked his stained mug of coffee down next to the olive-green phone and picked up the receiver. He looked at the rotary dial, looked at Robbie, looked back at the phone, and Robbie gulped. For a few anxious seconds, Robbie was sure Mr. Brewster was calling his parents! Does he know their number? Is he thinking it's too early, and calling might wake them up? The moments that passed seemed like days. Robbie was just about to turn and run when the man put the phone down. He rubbed his nose and his unshaven chin. He hooked his thumbs under his wide suspenders, lifted them up into the air, readjusted them around his shoulders, and let the elastic straps snap back against his massive chest.

"Okay," he rumbled.

On the opposite wall of the shack was a dirty, lopsided refrigerator that had once been white. A very large latch held the door shut. Mr. Brewster's meaty hand grabbed the latch and opened the heavy door. He slowly eased out a long, shallow cardboard box full of seaweed and handed it to Robbie. "Here you go," he said. "You can pick your own. Take a dozen of the big ones. They're the best." With a tremendous sense of relief, Robbie got to work.

Although sea worms and earth worms are pretty much the same in length and shape, sea worms have hundreds of little hairs on their sides that they use like legs to help them move around and dig holes in the mud to hide. Furthermore, they have two black pinchers in their mouths that they use to collect food, so they can really pinch when you pick them up the wrong way... OUCH!

One time, Robbie did an experiment. He didn't have any sea worms, so he went up behind the boatyard and dug a hole in the ground to get some earth worms to use for bait. The fish certainly knew the difference, as he didn't catch a thing that day!

George quickly shook his head in disbelief when he heard that story. He knew fish from the sea won't eat earth worms, and neither would he!

As Robbie chose the most promising sea worms, Mr.

Breaking the Rules

Brewster looked out the open door of the weathered shack. "Hey boy," he said with a chuckle and a grin. "There's a seagull in your boat!"

Robbie answered, "That's okay, it's just George, he's my friend."

"Your friend?" asked the man, looking over his glasses as he settled back into his broken chair with his coffee in hand. "A seagull?"

Robbie told him the story about meeting George. Mr. Brewster, looking puzzled, set his coffee down next to the radio and turned the volume down. He sat forward, right elbow on his right knee, chin propped up with his right hand, listening with interest, never blinking an eye. Robbie knew he didn't blink an eye because Mr. Brewster's glasses were so thick that they made his eyes look four times their real size.

Robbie looked up at the old clock on the wall, "Holy smokes!" he said as it read 12:00. While the clock was certainly broken, he realized he had been gone way too long. He fumbled for the quarter in his pocket to pay for the sea worms. Mr. Brewster stood up to put the cardboard box back into the refrigerator but noticed a big fat seaworm squirming in the seaweed. He turned around and looked at Robbie.

"Hey! Here you go," said Mr. Brewster, tossing him another worm. "This one's for your friend. Let's call it a baker's dozen!"

31

With a giant smile, Robbie handed Mr. Brewster his quarter and thanked him as he skipped out the door and down the dock.

Robbie, George and *Dolittle* made it back across the Piscataqua River safely, past the *Leonard W.* still tied to its dock, under the Navy Yard bridges, and all the way down the Back Channel to the little cove. With great relief, they anchored *Dolittle,* and Robbie smiled at George with satisfaction. His parents never even knew they were gone.

As time passed, Robbie and George fished together often. Seagulls love seafood, and while they will eat crabs, clams, mussels, snails and sea worms, George's favorite food was fish. He was a keen fisher. He would stand on his rock and wait for the tide to flow in or out. When it did, he knew that the mackerel, pollock, bluefish, and striped bass would chase the minnows up toward the surface and within his reach. When that happened, he'd spread his wings wide and, just at the right split second, he'd leap off the rock and swoop down to catch a fish. Sometimes he would sit right there in the water and swallow it whole and then be off again to catch another. Sometimes, if the fish was too big to eat on the spot, he'd

Breaking the Rules

hold it in his beak and fly it back to his rock to enjoy. One of his favorite things to do was to follow the lobstermen and fishing boats going in and out of the harbor, picking up scraps of fish and bait that fell from the boat into the water as the men worked. George was a very smart bird who learned by watching, as we all should.

When they fished together, George would tilt his head from side to side, watching the way Robbie fished with fascination. If you think about it from a seagull's perspective, people make things complicated. Fishermen like Robbie must get worms, buy hooks, put a worm on a hook, tie it to a line, attach it to a sinker and drop it into the water to attract fish. Sometimes he used his fishing pole. People must wear clothes, maybe even a jacket on cool mornings, and they often need raincoats and boots. Some people have boats with motors and need to mix oil and gas to make the motor run properly, or they need to use oars to row out to their favorite fishing spots. Then they need to take care of everything and maintain it. They need houses or boats to live in. They need cars. They need to work hard to make money to pay for everything, so they need jobs. George must have thought people were crazy! He had no such tools, no complications, no job, yet he was way more skilled and efficient at fishing than Robbie or anyone else.

Often, when they fished together, George would leap off the bow of *Dolittle*, dive into the water, catch a fish, eat it, and be perched back on the boat in the exact same spot

Robbie & George

within seconds, with no tools and nothing else required, not even a raincoat. What Robbie learned was this, think about it: George had nothing, yet he had everything. He had everything he needed. Life is simple for seagulls but for humans, life seemed complicated.

Robbie and George did almost everything together. Sometimes, on weekends, the Morin family would take *My Fair Lady* out to the Isles of Shoals, towing *Dolittle* behind. The Isles are about seven miles from Kittery; on a clear day you can see them from the mainland. They are a group of small rocky islands and tidal ledges. They all have names on the chart and the three largest islands are Appledore, Smuttynose, and Star. George always followed *My Fair Lady* there. He would fly way out ahead of the boat as if to lead the way and then circle back around to check on them, but he was never far away.

Robbie's dad brought along a milk crate. He would turn it upside down and let Robbie stand on it and steer *My Fair Lady*. He wanted Robbie to get the feel for steering a bigger boat, which Robbie did with great interest. When they got to the Isles of Shoals and moored *My Fair Lady* in the harbor, George would circle around them several times and land on the bow of *Dolittle*. He quickly shook his body, tilted his head from side to side, wiggled his wings as if to put them back in place and perched there looking at Robbie as if to say: "All right, what's next?"

George liked visiting the Isles of Shoals. There were many different types of seagulls there, and these seagulls

Breaking the Rules

all seemed to welcome him. Robbie learned later that the gulls on the Shoals were migratory birds, just passing through. George flew off to Appledore Island to visit with the other seagulls for a while. After everyone had lunch, George flew back to *Dolittle* and landed on the bow as usual. He looked at Robbie and his parents, wondering what they were doing and then, as if to say, "Come on let's go!" he flew off to nearby Smuttynose Island.

"George wants us to follow him!" Robbie pointed out. His parents gave him a skeptical look but went along with it.

George landed on the rooftop of a small, weathered cottage, so the Morins got into *Dolittle,* motored across the harbor and climbed up the path to the cottage. It was a quiet, beautiful spot. The unlocked door had a weathered sign that read "Welcome." When they knocked on the door, they noticed it was slightly open, so they slowly entered the cottage.

"Helloooo?" Mrs. Morin called. No one answered.

The little cottage was empty inside, and it smelled of wood, wild salty sea air, and of the wildflowers surrounding it. There was a guest book for visitors to sign, so they did. They noticed the other visitors who signed the book were from New Hampshire, Maine, Vermont, Massachusetts, New York and even London! How did they all get here? Robbie wondered.

The Morins spent an hour hiking around Smuttynose, enjoying the trails and salty air. It was a clear day, and the view was stunning. They could see all the way across the water to Kittery and Portsmouth. They could see Whaleback Lighthouse, the Wentworth Hotel, the prominent bridges in Portsmouth and even Mount Agamenticus in the distance. Occasionally, a harbor seal would swim by, poke his head up to check them out, then dive under again.

George, who was eager to show them more of the Isles, flew across Gosport Harbor to the big hotel on Star Island. Robbie and his parents watched George fly away, circle around the hotel two times, and land. They piled back into *Dolittle* and motored across the harbor to explore the beaches and the old stone buildings that line the little pathways of Star Island. At the hotel, they even bought ice cream cones: black raspberry for Mrs. Morin, chocolate as always for Mr. Morin, and mocha chip for Robbie. Robbie tossed George the very last bit of his cone to share. George had spent the whole day acting as if he was their tour guide and protector, leading them from island to island.

Breaking the Rules

As the weeks of summer passed, George became part of the family. Whenever they traveled to and from the Isles of Shoals, George followed them, circling *My Fair Lady*, soaring high in the air above them. George was always ahead of them and would be standing at the edge of the dock at Dion's, waiting for them to return.

Robbie's parents gave Robbie an allowance for doing chores around the boat. That meant making his bunk bed every morning, washing and cleaning *My Fair Lady*, and keeping *Dolittle* clean. He got extra money for catching fish for dinner so his mom didn't have to go to the grocery store. Robbie and George also used *Dolittle* to run a water taxi service. They shuttled people back and forth from the dock to their boats moored in the harbor. Doing that saved the boaters the trouble of rowing back and forth to their boats in their own smaller dinghies like Mr. and Mrs. Ellis did. The taxi service brought in some tips. Robbie's mom always made them a sandwich at lunchtime, but Robbie and George secretly agreed that when they saved up enough money, they were going to go on another adventure. Their plan was to pick the right day, the right time, take the tip money, speed down the Back Channel, go under the two Navy Yard Bridges, across the Piscataqua River again, and back to Portsmouth. Except this time it wasn't for sea worms, it was to treat themselves to lunch at Robbie's favorite sandwich shop, named Moe's.

The perfect day arrived. Robbie's mother was just

Robbie & George

about to make the daily sandwiches when Robbie said, "Thanks, Mom, but I'm not really hungry."

"Really? Not hungry? Well for heaven's sake, what's the world coming to? What about George?" she asked.

"Oh, I don't think he's hungry either," Robbie said.

She looked at him quizzically and muttered, "Hmmmmm... well, you know where the bologna and bread are."

Robbie ran to his bunk and grabbed the four quarters he had stashed away. He and George got into *Dolittle*, untied the lines, and pretended to go fishing. They went very slowly down the Back Channel toward one of their favorite fishing spots, where Robbie's parents were accustomed to seeing them. After a few minutes, they slipped past the *Green Can Number 5*, then the forbidden *Green Can Number 7*. They passed Gus Alley, standing on his dock. He waved to them, making a small, quick circular motion with his hand, a signal from Gus to "*rev it up*" so Robbie went faster and sped toward the Piscataqua River and across to Portsmouth they went. At Prescott Park, they tied the boat up to a fence post at the water's edge by Sheafe's Warehouse.

While George watched over the boat, Robbie climbed over the seawall. He ran up the hill to Moe's Sandwich Shop on Daniel Street to buy an Italian sandwich called a *Moe*. His family had been going there for years, but by car. Robbie ordered half a regular *Moe* with mayo and special oil, some Humpty Dumpty BBQ potato chips, and a Coke.

Breaking the Rules

The store was such a cool place. It was very narrow and deep, and the long line of customers formed in the shape of a U. You'd go in on the left side of the tiny store and then move with the line to the back of the store where you'd place your order. By the time you got back out towards the front where the cash register was, your sandwich would be ready. The line always moved right along, and the smell of the fresh bread, salami, cheese, onions, and green peppers drove Robbie crazy!

When it was time to pay, the man at the cash register said, "That will be $1.23, please." Uh-oh! Robbie knew he only had four quarters; he hadn't realized how much the sandwich would be. He fumbled through all his pockets just in case there was another coin or two. No such luck. The fast-moving line started to back up behind him, and the cashier called the owner of the shop over. It was Mr. Moe himself! He reached out his hand to Robbie, took the four quarters and remarked, "That will be enough this time, my friend."

Robbie thanked him very promptly, but he knew in his heart he would return someday with the 23 cents he owed Mr. Moe. He grabbed the goods and ran back to *Dolittle*, where George was still watching over the boat and waiting patiently.

Robbie & George

Breaking the Rules

Once his heartbeat slowed and he caught his breath, Robbie settled in to enjoy the food. The thick, fragrant Moe's was Robbie's all-time favorite sandwich. He often wished he could eat Moe's for school lunch back home, but Moe's only existed in Portsmouth. He flipped open his pocketknife and cut off bits and pieces of it to share with George. George loved Moe's too, except for the ring-shaped slices of onions and green peppers. He would pull them out with his sharp beak and push them aside. One by one, he'd pick them up, whirl them around like a hula hoop on his beak and toss them over the side of the boat. Then he'd watched them float away like it was some kind of game. It was funny to watch, and in a way, it was also like he was tidying up the boat, and teaching Robbie to do the same.

With their tummies satisfied, it was time to return to the boat yard. Robbie threw the lunch evidence in the trash can, tightened his lifejacket, untied the line, pulled on the starter rope and headed out across the Piscataqua River. He made sure he was well clear of the tanker ship that was steaming out of the harbor through the open Memorial Bridge towards the ocean. The freighter was assisted by two large, red tugboats, one on each side of the ship, and they both had a big white letter "P" on the sides of their smokestacks. They were sounding their loud, piercing whistles.

Robbie & George

Breaking the Rules

    This is how tugboats communicate. Because the tugs are on each side of the large ship, their ability to see each other is limited. So instead of visual communication like hand signals or voice communication, they use steam whistles on their smokestacks to signal each other on which way to tug the ship – to push, pull or turn. Because the river bends many times, ships could never negotiate their way to the ocean on their own, so the tugboats assist with this job. Robbie also saw two sailboats enjoying the fair breezes, and he made sure he stayed out of their way, too.

    Just as they were approaching the second Naval Yard bridge, a bright yellow lobster boat named *Limbo* came roaring toward *Dolittle*. It was Pete Patterson and his girlfriend, Carol. Robbie knew them because he had taken them from the dock out to their boat mooring just the day before. Clearly, Pete was showing off to Carol because he was paying no attention at all to the danger. It was up to Robbie to change course – and fast! He turned the wheel and gunned the motor so rapidly that George raised his wings high to keep his balance.

    "AWWWK!" called George.

    The wake of *Limbo* rocked *Dolittle* nearly on its side, and Robbie was glad his parents had taught him how to lean away from the waves and counterbalance the rough water as he steered.

    At last, they made it to the Back Channel, to their favorite little fishing spot in the cove next to *My Fair Lady*.

Robbie & George

Robbie tossed out the anchor, baited his hook and tossed that over the side too. He breathed a big sigh of relief and offered a sneaky grin towards George. After an hour or so of fishing, Robbie was convinced they had gotten away with it.

"Mission accomplished, George!"

The next few days were business as usual. Robbie spent all his time in *Dolittle*. The harbor was busy on the weekends, when folks who worked all week came to their boats.

One day, mid-week, Robbie and George were just tooling around the Back Channel when something caught their interest. Of course, it was outside their boundaries, (It seemed like all the best stuff was), but they couldn't resist. It was a submarine! Robbie steered slowly and carefully toward the Portsmouth Naval Shipyard, where he saw the *USS Sea Wolf* docked alongside the yard's pier. The *Sea Wolf* was enormous! With the top half of it out of the water, its conning tower and American flag flying high atop, the *Sea Wolf* rose far above *Dolittle*. Robbie was amazed!

He waved to the shipyard workers on the submarine,

Breaking the Rules

and they waved back to him. Curious, he got closer and closer. He had never seen a real working submarine this close before! He and George drifted alongside, staring at the submarine in awe, curious about every part of it. The sub was not only HUGE, but dark black and stealthy. Robbie wondered how the men lived inside it with no windows or portholes to see out of. How long could they live in there, under the water out in the ocean? Days? Weeks? Months? Where were the torpedoes? Were they ever used? Maybe his dad would know.

As fascinating as the *Sea Wolf* was, Robbie realized it was time to get going or his parents would be looking for him. He inched the throttle forward, gaining speed and motoring back towards *My Fair Lady*.

Suddenly, Robbie heard sirens and turned his head around. His eyes popped wide open at the sight of a large, black police boat with flashing blue lights and wailing sirens. It was speeding towards him! He heard a man calling him on the loudspeaker in a deep voice, "ATTENTION! ATTENTION! STOP!"

Robbie slowed *Dolittle* down to a crawl and put the throttle in neutral position. His heart was thumping hard. As the police pulled up alongside, Robbie could see the guns strapped around their waists. The men looked very big and important.

Breaking the Rules

Robbie raised his arms straight into the air. His mind raced. Oh no! he thought. They are going to kill me! (He was thinking of his parents, not the police.)

As the police approached, Robbie slowly lowered his shaking arms. The men were wearing thick, black vests. George was long gone; one smart bird, he likely flew away as soon as he saw the police boat coming at them. Both the police boat and *Dolittle* were drifting down river together with the current.

The Chief Officer asked, "What's your name?"

"Robbie," mustered Robbie.

"How old are you?" he asked.

"I'm nine," Robbie replied.

"He's nine," the officer said over the radio, then turned back to Robbie. "Where are you coming from?"

"Ahhhh... just over in the Back Channel."

"Did we see you crossing the Piscataqua earlier in the week?"

"Uhhhh, maybe. Probably. Yes, Sir." Robbie thought it was unwise to lie about that to the police.

"Where were you going the other day?"

"Moe's."

"Moe's? The sandwich shop?" The officer asked with surprise.

"Uh, yes Sir."

"And what are you doing here?"

"Looking at the submarine, Sir."

"Where do you live?"

Robbie & George

Robbie looked over his shoulder toward the boat yard.

"Just down the channel a bit at Dion's."

"You're living on one of those boats?"

"Yes, Sir."

"Which one?"

"*My Fair Lady*"

The officer made a note on his pad.

"Do your parents know you are here?"

"Uhhhh, no Sir."

"Well, at least I'm glad to see you have your life jacket on, Robbie."

By now, the police boat and *Dolittle* had drifted together, side by side, turning in slow circles due to the tidal currents. Robbie remembered his father teaching him about this current, and now he was caught in it, with a police boat next to him! They continued to drift under the second Navy Yard bridge and *My Fair Lady* was visible in the distance. Although the sirens and loudspeaker had stopped, the lights were still flashing. Robbie prayed his parents weren't watching. George was still nowhere in sight. Robbie thought, Some friend you are!

"Robbie," the officer asked, "do you know why we chased you?" He was sitting on the side of the police boat with his legs hanging over the side and his boots were on *Dolittle*'s rail, keeping the two vessels close together. There were two other officers standing behind him, both with guns in their holsters.

Breaking the Rules

"No, Sir. I wasn't speeding, was I?" Robbie gulped.

"You were on Federal Government waters back there, son, and so close to a nuclear submarine you could have touched it! You were so close that you triggered all the alarms on the Naval Base. We are not the local police, we're the Federal Police and here to protect the Navy Yard. When everyone on the base heard the alarms go off, we rushed over. Look behind you!"

Robbie tuned his head to see two additional police boats approaching them from the opposite direction. The three boats, with lights still flashing, surrounded *Dolittle*, and all were drifting down the channel closer and closer to *My Fair Lady*. The officers were talking back and forth to each other on their VHF radios, explaining the situation and Robbie's stomach was in knots from all of the commotion.

At that point, the other boats turned off their flashing lights. One of the police boats turned around and headed back up the channel. The second one soon followed.

"Well, here's what I think," the officer said. "We could arrest you and bring you into the Navy Yard Prison for questioning and impound your boat. Do you know what impound means?"

"No, Sir, I don't."

"It means we could take your boat away from you forever."

Oh no! thought Robbie. Not *Dolittle*!!

"But I don't think your parents would be too happy

about that, do you?"

Robbie nodded vigorously. "No, no, I agree. They would not be happy about that at all."

As they were spun slowly around in circles by the currents, Robbie kept looking over the officer's shoulder at *My Fair Lady* with all the hatches and windows open but no sign of his parents.

"Well, I think you should be on your way," the officer said. "The only potential threat you can be around here is to the bottom fish with that hand line you have there. But listen to me and listen to your parents, always wear your life jacket, and NEVER, EVER get that close to a submarine again, do you understand me?"

"Yes Sir, I do," Robbie said. "I promise."

The officer used his feet to push the two boats apart from one another so they could move on. As they separated, he called out "What's the name of your little boat?"

"*Dolittle,* Sir, as in *Dr. Dolittle* the movie."

And the officer replied, "That's a good name... we'll be seeing you around, Robbie." The two other officers waved good-bye.

The police boat turned around and followed the other two police boats up the river and away from *My Fair Lady*.

Robbie almost passed out! He inhaled deeply and let out a huge sigh of relief. PHEW! What had just happened? He was shaking, and the palms of his hands were all sweaty as he tried to grip the steering wheel. He motored very slowly back to the boat yard, needing time to think. He pulled in, tied up *Dolittle,* and sat on the dock next to the other boats thinking about everything and trying to think about nothing. Out of nowhere, George landed on the dock next to Robbie. He quickly shook his body, tilted his head from side to side, wiggled his wings as if to put them back in place and stood there looking at Robbie as if to say: "All right, what's next?"

"George!! Where have you been!?" Robbie exclaimed. "I almost got arrested and *Dolittle* was nearly impounded!! You missed it!" George said nothing, and just eyed the outgoing tide, looking for jumping fish.

"And thankfully," Robbie added, "Mom and Dad never even knew what happened!"

Under Suspicion

The next day, Robbie and his parents drove to Portsmouth in their car instead of using *Dolittle*. They went to Strawbery Banke, an outdoor walking museum depicting life and times back in the 18th century. They strolled among the historic buildings, crossed the street toward the harbor, and entered Prescott Park, where an arts festival was underway. There they walked through the many flower gardens that were bursting with purples, yellows, oranges and reds. Robbie glanced over at the Sheafe Warehouse and saw the little knoll and fence post he tied *Dolittle* to just a few days earlier when he went to Moe's. He wondered, and worried a little, if his parents knew what he had done.

Naaahhh, he thought. But just then they turned in the direction of the Sheafe Warehouse.

"Mom, where are we going?" asked Robbie nervously.

"Along the river, to the Sheafe Warehouse," she replied, as they stepped closer to the fence post.

"Isn't it a beautiful day, Robbie?" she asked. "Just look

Under Suspicion

how calm the river is. Even little boats like *Dolittle* could cross it on a day like today, don't you think?"

Robbie gulped. His eyes widened and his heart began to beat faster. He knew he was never supposed to go past *Green Can Number 7* in the Back Channel. They had warned him about that over and over. Did his mom know? Was she leading him to confess? He thought about being grounded for the rest of the summer and not being allowed to use *Dolittle* again, but then he thought even harder about not thinking about it... at least for now!

The good news was that his mom was smiling and seemed happy. So far, so good! Right? Maybe she won't ask, Robbie hoped. Mr. and Mrs. Morin turned away from the river toward the Sheafe Warehouse. That day it housed part of the art show.

Out of the corner of his eye, Robbie saw the head of a seagull peeking out from around the corner of the building. It wasn't just any seagull, it was George! He was standing on the seawall just behind the old wooden building, watching out for them as he normally did (likely hoping for another piece of Moe's).

Robbie knew George could not talk, but he was afraid that George's presence would somehow reveal their previous adventures. That was silly, but sometimes feeling guilty can make you think silly things. Robbie thought if he could somehow shoo George away, his parents would not be suspicious of what he did, and everything would be okay. He slowed behind his parents, discreetly waving his arms, motioning for George to go away. He whispered under his breath so his parents wouldn't hear. "What are you doing here? You're not supposed to be here... you need to go home! Go! Get outta here!" Robbie's facial expression and wide eyes alone should have sent George flying.

Robbie's mom turned around and looked at him. "What's wrong? Did you see a ghost?"

"Oh no!" he said, straightening up his posture. He looked in the opposite direction at the flower gardens, trying to distract her view of George. "Everything is fine, I'm fine. Like you said, it's a beautiful day! Look at those flowers, Mom!" Half of him was trying to shoo George away, but the other half thought it was cool that George had followed the family car all the way into Portsmouth. George, after all, was curious, and Robbie realized it was no use to try and shoo him away. George will do what George wants to do.

The Morins entered the Sheafe Warehouse to see the beautiful paintings. The small building was built in the early 1700s. It sits out alongside the water and was once used to lift cargo onto and out of small ships. John Paul Jones, a naval commander in the Revolutionary War, used it for loading cargo onto the famous Navy sailing Sloop-of-War ship, the *USS Ranger*. The warehouse had been restored to its original charm and was used for all sorts of exhibits.

On this day, there was a prominent lady standing at

Under Suspicion

the entrance greeting visitors. Robbie was looking at George, who was still peeking his head around the corner. He was motioning as discreetly as he could for George to buzz off. The lady at the door watched Robbie's peculiar behavior. As soon as he became aware she was looking at him, he stopped gesturing at George, and stared at her instead. He had never seen anyone like her before. She was certainly an important person because she wore her hair up in a bun and she had on a beautiful white ruffled dress with hoops in it. Robbie had never seen a dress like that before, or at least, had never seen his mother wear anything like that. Robbie pointed at her dress and asked if it was held out by hula hoops.

She laughed. "No Dear, I'm dressed in period clothing. It is what would have been worn by women back in the 1700s. My name is Rose Labrie. What's your name?"

"Robbie," he answered, immediately put at ease by her friendly manner. Mrs. Labrie was the famous artist who had painted all the artwork on display in the building. Not only was her name Rose, she even had a big, fresh, red rose pinned to her dress.

Under Suspicion

Mrs. Labrie welcomed Robbie and his parents in and walked them through her exhibit, telling them a bit about each of her paintings. The paintings depicted little towns, skaters on frozen ponds, summer farm life, a bear in the woods, horses trotting through snow, and many other happy scenes. After his mom and dad talked with Mrs. Labrie for a few minutes, they wandered off to look at the other exhibits outside on the lawn, but Robbie stayed with her.

He was fascinated by her painting of the *USS Thresher*, a submarine that was lost at sea not far from Portsmouth. All 129 sailors aboard drowned in the tragedy on April 10, 1963. Mrs. Labrie made a large painting of it in their memory. The painting showed dark clouds in a red and orange threatening sky, the top of the submarine awash in white water, and all 129 names of the sailors were painted in white letters over the deep black and blue sea beneath the submarine. Below the names were the words *Asleep in the Deep*. He shivered as he stared at each name. He was too young to know anything about that tragedy or any of the brave men aboard, but the thought of so many people drowning in the cold, dark water, trapped inside a big machine, disturbed him. Robbie had a newfound respect for the Navy Yard, the people who worked there, and the men who served in the Navy on those submarines.

Robbie moved along to look at a colorful and fun painting called *The Red Sleigh*, showing children skating

Robbie & George

on a pond with a horse and sleigh riding past. The pond was called the "Puddle Dock" and was just across the street from where they were standing.

Oh no! Robbie thought when he glanced out the window. It was George again! This time George was standing on the sill of the open window, peeking in. Robbie walked towards the window, about to shoo him away and off the ledge, but he noticed Mrs. Labrie walking toward him, so he turned his attention toward her instead.

She told Robbie more about her folk-art paintings, including the *USS Thresher*. A lot of nine-year-olds wouldn't have been interested, but Robbie sure was. Her stories and paintings fascinated him so much that he asked her if she would paint a painting for him.

"Well," she said with a big smile, "I'd consider it, but what would you like a painting of?"

"Hmmmm, good question. I'd have to think about it," he said and didn't answer right away. He walked around, looked at her paintings, looked outside at the festival, and thought about what he would like the painting to be of. He walked over to the window and looked at George.

Mrs. Labrie continued to greet visitors and hand out leaflets. Robbie decided to take a chance and said, "I've got it! Me and my best friend!"

"What's that?" Mrs. Labrie asked, a bit startled. Her mind had moved on to other matters.

"Well, the painting! You asked me what I'd like to have

Under Suspicion

a painting of. Would you paint me a painting of me and my best friend?"

She looked interested again and with a grin asked, "What's your friend's name?"

"George!" he said.

"Oh, well I see... do you have a photo of George?" she asked. "It would be a lot easier to paint a painting of him if I knew what he looked like."

"Hmmmm, good point." He thought for a minute and said, "No, I don't have a photo of George."

"And where is George?" she asked. Just then, nosey George poked his head in the window and back out again before he flew down onto the lawn alongside the building.

Robbie giggled and said confidently, "He's just outside." Mrs. Labrie walked to the door in her white hooped dress and looked outside.

"Outside?" she asked curiously.

She looked to the right, to the left, and then turned around and looked at Robbie, "I don't see anyone out there," she said. "He must be with your parents," and shrugged her shoulders. She looked around again and said, "I only see a seagull."

"That's him!" said Robbie with a grin.

"A seagull?" she asked, looking surprised.

"Yes!" Robbie said proudly. "His name is George, and he is my best friend! He rides with me in *Dolittle*."

"What's *Dolittle*?"

Robbie & George

"*Dolittle* is my boat! George likes to stand up on the bow. We go fishing together all the time over in the Back Channel and..." Robbie caught himself from saying anything more. He didn't want to admit to all the things he and George had done that were against the rules.

When his mom and dad came looking for Robbie, Mrs. Labrie informed them that she and Robbie had reached an "agreement." His parents were very surprised at what had transpired within a few minutes of leaving Robbie alone with Mrs. Labrie. She explained to them that she would create a painting of Robbie and his best friend George, and from that day on, Robbie promised to save all his money until Christmas in exchange for the painting. He would have to work extra hard and earn a lot of money, because he could see that her paintings were worth way more than he could afford.

They all thanked her very much. They left the building and Robbie followed his parents back to the car. As they crossed the street to the parking lot, he looked back and saw Rose Labrie standing in the doorway, waving goodbye. George was standing right next to her, watching them walk away too. Mrs. Labrie looked down at George and George looked up at her. In Robbie's mind, the two of them had become friends, and Mrs. Labrie thought George was one most unusual seagull.

As they drove home to *My Fair Lady*, Robbie was smiling broadly. From the back seat he could see George flying alongside the Memorial Bridge and down into the

Back Channel, above the *USS Seawolf*, over the second bridge towards the boat yard. When they reached *My Fair Lady*, George flew down and landed on the dock. He quickly shook his body, tilted his head from side to side, wiggled his wings as if to put them back in place and stood there looking at all of them as if to say: "All right, what's next?"

The Water Taxi

The little water taxi business grew and grew as the summer heated up and more people came to their boats. They would drive to the boatyard on weekends with carloads of groceries and marine supplies. Loading these items into their little dinghies to row to their moored boats was a hassle. This is why they used Robbie's shuttle service.

Most of the dinghies were rowboats, meaning they had no outboard engine so one would have to row with oars. *Dolittle*, being a Boston Whaler and unsinkable, was more substantial, very stable, and had an engine. *Dolittle* was always tied up to the dock next to *My Fair Lady*. There were only about a half dozen dock slips available at Dion's for the summer season, with a long waiting list. To make space for more boaters, Dion's added moorings out in the harbor. A mooring has 3 parts to it: a large cement block (or a mushroom-shaped anchor) that lies on the

Caught in the Act

seabed, a large ball that floats on the surface with a floating mooring line, and a chain that connects the two. A boater would tie the floating mooring line to the bow of his or her boat to secure it in the harbor. Each boater knew which mooring was theirs.

One benefit of a mooring is that they are less expensive to rent; however, you need to have a dinghy to get back and forth from the boats to the shore. Boaters with moorings could also use the marina's amenities (things like the dinghy dock, showers, trash removal, the parking lot, etc.). Boaters on moorings appreciated the quick shuttle service Robbie offered. It was easy and convenient. If they only came to their boats on weekends, sometimes their dinghies, which were tied to the dock, would be full of rainwater which needed bailing. This was another job Robbie took up, bailing out the dinghies before the boaters arrived.

Everyone referred to the water taxi business as "Robbie's" because George always flew away when there was too much commotion with people and their bags. Robbie kept an eye on George and often, when customers came aboard, they'd ask, "How's George doing?"

"Great!" Robbie would say. "He's right over there," and he would point to George, who was standing on his rock or on his piling, watching from a comfortable distance.

Robbie happily loaded his customers' bags into *Dolittle* and took them out to their boats. This was how he earned

Robbie & George

his tip money. Robbie talked to George about having a set fee of twenty-five cents per trip, but George shook his head from side to side and apparently didn't like that idea too much, because sometimes people tipped them even more than a quarter!

With special permission and instructions from his mom and dad, Robbie delivered people across the Piscataqua River at the south end of the Back Channel. They would go toward the Portsmouth Yacht Club in New Castle, visible from *My Fair Lady* and within sight of Robbie's parents. A couple of times Robbie had permission to take the Sterling or the Johnson families all the way around the corner, out of sight, eastward to Pepperrell Cove, Frisbee's General Store, and Captain Simeon's Galley Restaurant. His parents knew the Johnsons and Sterlings would be able to help if Robbie got into a pinch. Customers tipped him to be dropped off to shop at the store or eat at the restaurant, and then tipped again when he picked them up.

One time, he was asked to take some empty fuel jugs over to the Portsmouth Yacht Club to have them filled. He got an extra tip for this service! All of Robbie's customers seemed to know that Robbie was saving up for a special painting by Rose Labrie.

As the summer went on, Robbie and George kept busy by fishing or just slowly riding around the harbor in *Dolittle* but on Fridays, they would get ready for the people to arrive by car. *Dolittle* was always clean and

Caught in the Act

waiting at the dock for those needing a lift to their boats.

One of their customers was named Holly. Her blonde hair was braided like a chain of pretzels, her blue eyes were bright, and she always had a suntan. She was an accomplished sailor and lived alone on her sailboat in the harbor. She usually rowed in and out to her sailboat for exercise, but when it was raining or cold, she would ask Robbie to take her back and forth, and she tipped him well.

Dr. Lux was an old curmudgeon and never tipped. He was even older than his old wooden boat, *Morning Star*. His parking spot was the farthest one from the docks, and his boat was the last mooring ball out in the Back Channel.

One Saturday night during dinner aboard *My Fair Lady*, Robbie slumped down into his seat with a heavy sigh.

"What's wrong with you?" asked his father.

"Dad, I like all my customers, but Dr. Lux is tough."

"How so?" he asked.

"He's old, and doggone it, I go all the way up the hill to his car to get all of his things," Robbie grumbled. "I load his grocery bags, ice, books, charts, flashlights, tools—whatever he has—into a cart. I lug it all the way down to the dock and put it into *Dolittle*. Then, I take Dr. Lux and all his stuff out to his boat and I unload everything onto the deck of *Morning Star*. Then I have to help Dr. Lux onto the boat, being very careful so he doesn't slip. He gripes at me the whole time and…"

"Now son…," said his father.

"Sometimes I put his stuff away for him," Robbie continued without taking a breath., "wherever he says to, and he barks out orders, 'Ice goes in the fridge! Wrench goes in the tool drawer! No not that drawer, the other one!'"

"Hold on, Robbie!'" said his father, raising up his hand to try to interrupt.

"Then I do it all over again on Sunday in the reverse. He never gives me a tip, ever," Robbie continued, getting louder. "Not even a doggone nickel!"

"Son!" said his father, also getting louder.

Robbie gulped some milk before continuing. "I just don't understand why the car of the oldest person in the boat yard has to be the farthest away in the parking lot, and his boat is the farthest away in the harbor, and he just keeps bossing me around. It's just not fair!" Robbie said with a snort.

"ROBERT W MORIN THE THIRD!" said his mother loudly, as she loaded the plates with Slumgullion. "Your father can't get a word in edgewise. Be quiet, would you?"

Robbie scowled at the homemade food, even though he loved it, and slumped back down again.

His father continued in between bites. "Son, brace yourself. Sometimes life is not all about you, imagine that? Sometimes life is all about other people. In this case,

Caught in the Act

it's about helping other people, especially those who cannot help themselves. Dr. Lux cannot row all the way out to his boat, especially against the tides and currents, which you know can be very strong. It is much easier for him to park up the hill, where there is more space for him to turn his car around. You should just focus on helping people. A tip is exactly that, a tip, and these folks do not owe you anything. You are helping others and that is what always counts in the end. If you get a tip, YOU should thank THEM."

Robbie sat doodling sailboats and connecting the dots on a Dairy Queen place mat, acting as if he wasn't listening but hearing every single word.

"Dr. Lux appreciates your help, Robbie, he just has a funny way of showing it," his mother said. "Just keep helping him, and the rest of the folks, too. You are doing a fantastic job and you're a better person to be doing what you're doing. Patience is a virtue we should all practice and you should practice it too. Treat Dr. Lux with respect and patience."

"Okay, okay I get it." Robbie said, calming down.

"Well then," his mom said, "finish your dinners, we have brownies for dessert, I just made them this morning. Last one to finish does the dishes!"

Robbie emptied his plate into his mouth and said, laughing with food coming out, "Guess that means you, Dad!"

The five members of the Johnson family were perhaps

Robbie & George

Robbie's favorite water taxi customers. He couldn't wait for them to get to the boat yard so he could help them. They had the most beautiful sailboat, named *Magic*. Besides Mr. and Mrs. Johnson, there were three kids near Robbie's age — Christina, Hastings, and Nathan— and they were all friendly and fun. When they weren't out sailing on *Magic*, they would hang out in the harbor.

Robbie loved going over to their boat, whether for breakfast, lunch, dinner, or sometimes just to play with the kids. On rainy days, the kids would play games inside the boat like Monopoly, Parcheesi, or Go Fish. Admittedly, the girls were always best at the games. On nice days, they would jump off the bow of their sailboat and go swimming. Nathan always did the best cannonballs.

Other times they all got into *Dolittle* and went for a ride to the beach across the harbor. There they could pick mussels and dig clams for dinner, or just collect shells. All the while, George was nearby. The Johnsons thought George was great and were amazed at how Robbie interacted with him. Robbie was always sorry to see them go home on Sundays, and he could hardly wait to see them again the following weekend.

One Sunday evening, right after he said goodbye to the Johnsons, he returned to *My Fair Lady* for dinner. His mom was just putting one of his favorite meals on the plates: grilled hot dogs on toasted buns topped with relish and mustard... YUM!

Caught in the Act

"You look very thoughtful," she observed.

"Well, you know, Mom," Robbie said, "you and Dad are right. The Johnsons didn't tip me today. They usually tip, and this time they didn't. They probably forgot. But I thought about what you and Dad said. It doesn't matter that they forgot. I didn't say anything to them because I was happy to help. I got more out of just being with them and I can't wait to see them again next weekend and to help with anything they need. They are so nice to me and they let George tag along, too."

Robbie's Mother beamed with happiness. "That's so nice to hear you say Robbie, I'm really proud of you."

Oftentimes, when Robbie took people to Pepperrell Cove, there would be a dozen little sailboats sailing all around him. Because Robbie was in a motorboat, he had to "give way" to the sailboats and let them pass in front. It's harder to control a sailboat than a motorboat. This is why sailboats have the "right of way" over motorboats, another important rule his parents taught him. With fascination, Robbie watched the kids in the sailboats tacking back and forth. He decided that someday he wanted to learn how to sail.

Robbie & George

One day, after he dropped the Browns at Pepperrell Cove, he tied *Dolittle* up to the dock and told George to watch over the boat. Robbie took off his life jacket, walked up the ramp, along the pier, and down the stairs next to Captain Simeon's Restaurant. In the lower level of that building there was a sailing school at the Kittery Point Yacht Club. Inside, a woman greeted him.

He said, "Hi! My name is Robbie and I'd like to learn how to sail." She was very friendly, but she said the lessons were booked for the rest of the summer and she mentioned that he'd need his parents approval anyway. She gave him a flyer and said she could reserve a spot for him for the following summer. When he got back to *My Fair Lady* he gave the information to his mom and dad.

They looked the information over and said, "We'll see."

Robbie felt that when parents say, "We'll see," it really means "no." Or does it?

Robbie's mom and dad were developing more and more confidence and trust in Robbie's ability to run *Dolittle*. They were comfortable with Robbie going beyond his boundaries when he was taxiing people around and helping his customers and knew he was saving his money for the painting. Many of the customers' destinations were out of his parents' sight, and beyond Robbie's boundaries, but they became comfortable with that. After his mom and dad gave their consent, Robbie and George even went all the way around Seavey Island alone, including around the whole Naval Shipyard, which was an accomplishment to be proud of!

So maybe next year his parents *would* let him take sailing lessons, and maybe they'd let him cross the river on his own. Robbie new he was old enough, and responsible enough. He'd done it already, all by himself, even though it was against the rules. He was definitely ready!

Caught in the Act

A quiet weekday arrived when there were no customers, and all the chores were done. Robbie said, "George! What do you think?" eyeballing *Dolittle*.

George tilted his head from side to side and wiggled his wings in agreement. Fishing was his kind of thing, and he was always ready for more. He waddled across the dock to *Dolittle* and hopped aboard to join Robbie. The only problem was that they did not have any sea worms, and Robbie's parents were away grocery shopping. Despite the recent expansion of his boundaries, Robbie did not want to take the chance of violating his mom and dad's growing trust and confidence in his seamanship. He didn't want to go back across the Piscataqua River to Brewster's Bait Shop without asking. Plus, the river's current looked fast and furious that day.

"I've got an idea!" Robbie said to George. "Instead of going to Brewster's, let's go dig our own sea worms!"

The tide was going out and it would be low tide soon, so they could dig in the muddy bottom along the shore.

Caught in the Act

But they had to hurry. The tide was really ripping through the river that day because of the full moon. Robbie knew that the phase of the moon controls the tides, which controls how fast the water moves, which way it goes, how much water moves, and when. The gravity pull of a full moon has more force than other phases, moving more water, and faster. Tide charts are created based on the phase of the moon and all smart mariners and fishermen study the tide charts before they get underway.

Robbie said, "Let's go George!"

He ran back to *My Fair Lady* and rummaged through his closet for his rubber boots. He grabbed the peanut butter & jelly sandwiches his mom had left for them and away they went in *Dolittle*. They headed around the corner and into Spruce Creek, a large, shallow body of water they had never explored before. Robbie had seen it from the car while crossing the Whipple Road Bridge though and thought it would be a great place to find sea worms. The digging is fun, but it must be done quickly before the tide turns and the water comes back in, flooding the muddy bottom.

Robbie found the perfect spot up Spruce Creek, just past the bridge. They set out the anchor and made sure it was secure. He lifted the outboard engine so the propeller would not get stuck in the mud. Then he swung his legs overboard, grabbed his bait bucket and started digging. He lifted the seaweed up and sure enough, there were a few sea worms underneath. He grabbed them and threw them into the bucket. He did it again with another patch of seaweed. George stood nearby, watching; it was a trick George had always known.

Robbie was so enthralled in finding the worms under the seaweed, laughing at George, and just enjoying the fun that he forgot about the tide. It was coming in quickly, and the water would soon cover his boots if he didn't hurry. Satisfied with all the worms he had caught, he grabbed onto *Dolittle's* rail and lifted himself up and over the side, swinging his muddy boots into the boat. The worms were secured, and George was ready to go. Robbie tossed George a worm and chuckled as he slurped it down with one gulp. Then he helped himself to a pb&j sandwich. "Okay George, let's go catch some fish!"

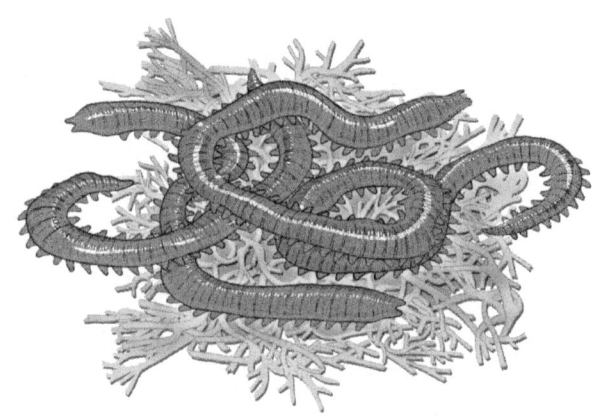

Caught in the Act

Robbie lowered the engine down so the propeller was back in the water and pulled the starter cord. Nothing. He pulled again. Nothing. Just a small rumble, but it wouldn't start. He pulled again and again and again. Worry set in. Robbie took off the engine cover like he saw his dad do once but wasn't sure what to look for.

"Why won't it start?!" he groaned. "Come ooonnnn!!"

He put the engine cover back on and pulled again and again, gritting his teeth. The tide was coming in and he knew no one would ever think to look for him in Spruce Creek, beyond the Whipple Road Bridge. A few more unsuccessful pulls on the cord made Robbie slump down onto his knees, burying his face in his hands. When he uncovered his face, he saw the red gas tank.

UH OH... OH NOOOO! he thought. He lifted it up and sure as shooting, it was empty. He even opened it and looked inside. Yep, it was empty alright, it was bone dry. He felt helpless and angry with himself. He had gone beyond *Red Nun Number 4* and past *Green Can Number 3* all by himself. In his rush to get underway, he forgot to check the gas tank. Not only that, but he also forgot his life jacket. He had broken all the rules. He was not safe and worse — he was going to be in trouble!

"How could I be so stupid?" he asked George. George gave him one of those looks.

They were in a real pickle. Mr. and Mrs. Morin were away from home, and *Dolittle* and her crew were stuck in the middle of nowhere with no gas, nobody ashore, nor

Robbie & George

anyone in a boat to signal for help. There was no getting out of this mess and no way to explain it. They forgot about the worms and fishing.

The wind picked up and the temperature dropped, foretelling a storm was on the way.

"Oh boy," cried Robbie. "How could this get any worse?"

George didn't answer.

The clouds in the distance were big and purple. Robbie didn't know what to do. The tide was coming in fast, creating a very strong current. He had oars, but he certainly wasn't strong enough to row back to the boat yard against both the storm and the current. George looked worried. He paced back and forth around *Dolittle's* perimeter, barely keeping his balance, and pooping all over *Dolittle*. Robbie had never seen George poop this much before!

"We must be in really awful trouble if you're this worried," Robbie told George.

Indeed, the skies darkened, turning a darker purplish gray. A loud boom of thunder made him shutter. Within a few minutes it was pouring rain. The wind continued to howl, the little ripples turned into small waves, the small waves continued to get bigger. Robbie had no slicker, but he laid down on the narrow seat in the aft section of *Dolittle* and pulled the canvas boat cover over himself. *Dolittle* bounced around while the anchor luckily held fast.

Caught in the Act

George was standing on the bow in the pouring rain, wondering why Robbie was hiding under a cover. George himself had his feathers for protection and if you think about it, he was essentially waterproof and coldproof too! He was happy just closing his eyes and standing in the storm. It reminded Robbie again of just how simple and uncomplicated George's life was. For a seagull, a rainstorm was just a showering. Plus, George could always fly anywhere for shelter if he really wanted to. The bolts of lightning lit up the dark sky, followed by more thunder. Robbie lifted up the boat cover and called to George, "Come on, get under the cover!"

George opened his closed eyes and peered at Robbie for a second. He wasn't too keen on the idea of getting under the cover and instead waddled down into the boat to get out of the wind, where he stood guard for Robbie outside the cover, keeping a watchful eye on the sky. As the rainwater began to accumulate and make big puddles in the boat, Robbie knew he had to start bailing, but the rain, wind and thunder were too much for him to deal with at that moment. George, on the other hand, seemed unaffected by the water, standing happily knee deep in the puddles. His legs, knees and big yellow, webbed feet were like rubber, no need for boots! The cover served as good protection for Robbie against the stinging rain, so he decided to stay put until the storm let up.

Instead, the weather worsened. The gusty winds were making the sea rough, and the waves turned into whitecaps. The rain turned to hail, at first the size of peas and then the size of golfballs! The storm seemed endless, but luckily the anchor continued to hold, preventing *Dolittle* from being smashed against rocks, or blown over. Robbie was so scared he was shaking, partly from the immediate danger, and partly from knowing he should not have been there in the first place and was going to be in trouble. Eventually, the heavy rain eased up and the lightning and thunder finally passed. George waddled out again through the water and across the balls of hail to his favorite spot on the bow. He quickly shook his body, tilted his head from side to side, wiggled his wings as if to put them back in place and stood there looking at Robbie, in what was left of the rainstorm, as if to say: "All right, what's next?"

Robbie got out from under the cover and saw all the water in *Dolittle*. He grabbed the bailer — which was made from an old plastic bleach bottle, cut in half — and started to scoop out the water and hail balls. His clothes were soaked, and his body was shivering from the cold. George was puzzled by the whole thing, but he knew that something was not right.

It was getting late in the afternoon and the sun was setting in the western sky. There was no way for Robbie to call his mom and dad or send a signal to anyone that he and George were there. There were still no boats passing by, and he couldn't see any houses along the shore, only woods. Robbie and George were alone and

Caught in the Act

helpless. George, sensing something was wrong, paced back and forth across the bow of the boat, stomping his feet as if thinking of a solution to the problem. Then, to Robbie's distress, George flew away.

"HEY! WAIT! DON'T GO NOW!" Robbie yelled, but off George went. Robbie felt lonelier than ever before. His only friend had deserted him, even though *he* had always been loyal to George.

Meanwhile, Robbie's parents had been caught in the same thunderstorm as they returned with the groceries in their car. It was raining so hard they pulled off to the side of the road for a while before continuing to the boatyard. By then the storm had passed and George met them right on the forward deck of *My Fair Lady*.

"Hey George!" exclaimed Robbie's mom in surprise. She almost dropped the wet bag of groceries his dad was handing over to her from the dock. They took a moment to watch George walk nervously back and forth across the deck, something they'd never seen him do before.

While Robbie's mom started unpacking groceries, his dad knelt near George and asked, "What's wrong, Friend? Are you hungry?" Seagulls are almost always

Robbie & George

hungry, so that was a good guess. He opened the box of sea worms he had picked up for Robbie as part of the shopping list, and he offered one to George. George refused it, and instead kept pacing back and forth, back and forth, now pooping all over the deck of *My Fair Lady*, which had never happened before. Mr. Morin dropped the sea worm back in the box and scratched his head. "I don't know what's wrong with George," he called down below to his wife, Betsy. "He's acting very strange."

When Mrs. Morin came up from the galley to call Robbie to dinner, she looked around, but didn't see *Dolittle*. George was acting more distressed all the time, pacing around, then flying off a little way and returning, again and again.

"Where can that boy be?" his mother wondered. The storm had only just ended, so he couldn't have been on the water for long.

She cupped her hands and called out, "Robbie! ROBBIE!" But there was no answer. "Bob," she called to her husband, "both Robbie and *Dolittle* are gone and not within sight."

At the sound of her call, heads popped out from other nearby rain-soaked boats. She strode quickly along all the docks, asking everyone, but nobody else had seen Robbie either.

Finally, Mr. Plager, the owner of *Compass Rose*, said, "Why don't you ask George?"

"Huh? What do you mean?" she replied with a

Caught in the Act

puzzled look.

"Well, if anyone knows where Robbie is, chances are it would be George, right?" he said.

She looked at him with a smile and hurried back to *My Fair Lady*. She clutched her husband's hand as he helped her get aboard the boat. "Come with me!" she said to Bob.

They awkwardly stepped toward George on the bow of the boat, kneeling to his level, feeling a bit foolish talking to a seagull. Anxiously, Mrs. Morin asked, "Where's..." and in a split-second George took flight, before she could even say Robbie's name.

He flew low in the air and out of the harbor and around the corner into Spruce Creek and back again. Mr. Morin figured it was a sign and said, "My God! That's it! That's where he is. He must be in trouble in Spruce Creek!" They considered calling the Coast Guard, but there was no time.

"Oh, Bob!" his wife exclaimed. "He must have been caught in that horrible storm, let's go!" The boat yard has a small motorboat, called a launch, available for their workers to use during working hours, and for their customers to use after hours. The Morins did not hesitate to use it without asking as this was an emergency!

They had become accustomed to George leading the way, and he was on the job this time, circling around them, soaring across the river, turning left into Spruce Creek and back out again. He was, after all, a most unusual seagull. He circled above Robbie and *Dolittle*, then flew back out to the harbor and over the speeding launch. The launch was fast, but George was much faster and able to fly in front of it. He made the circuit several times, until the launch passed under the Whipple Road Bridge. From there, they could just make out *Dolittle*, anchored in the distance, off to the side of the channel, with George circling above it.

Robbie was sitting there all alone, shivering, wrapped in the canvas and trying to stay warm, when he heard the buzzing of a boat engine. He got out from underneath the cover and stood up and waved, crisscrossing his arms in the air, signaling an emergency... exactly what his parents had taught him to do. A sense of relief flooded over him as he saw it was his mom and dad, with George leading the way. His parents spotted Robbie and sped toward him. Just as they pulled up alongside *Dolittle*, George shot down from high in the air and landed precisely on his favorite spot, *Dolittle's* bow. He quickly shook his body, tilted his head from side to side, wiggled his wings as if to put them back in place and stood there looking at the three of them as if to say: "I can't wait to see this!"

George watched with interest as all three of them took a deep breath. Robbie's father sat on the side of the boatyard launch with his legs draped over the side and his feet on *Dolittle,* keeping the two boats together much like the way the Navy Yard police officer had done.

Caught in the Act

Robbie & George

The look of both relief and disappointment on Mr. Morin's face spoke volumes. Sometimes, especially at times like this, saying everything says nothing but saying nothing says everything.

He looked across the harbor and off into the distance in thought. He looked down at his hands resting in his lap, with fingers intertwined and cracking his knuckles, just thinking, cautiously thinking.

After a deep inhale and exhale, he looked at Robbie and very quietly asked the question...

"So. What happened?"

Taking time to answer, "I ran out of gas," Robbie said quietly, with his head hung low.

More time passed.

"And where is your life jacket?" his mother asked.

Robbie looked away in disgust "Um, I...I forgot it," he muttered.

His father said, "You're alone, and you've gone beyond your boundaries."

Robbie sighed, "Yes, I know."

His father asked, "Just curious, do you have anything to say for yourself?"

Robbie looked around, and gulped. "I'm sorry," he said in a low voice. "I'm really, really sorry and I won't ever do this again." He knew he had broken all the rules but most importantly, he had disappointed his parents. They had been so nice to allow him to use *Dolittle* all summer long, and he had really let them down.

Caught in the Act

As good parents do, his mom and dad looked at him, saying nothing more, but thinking in silence. They did not yell, nor did they pile on scornful remarks. They simply gave him a long, long, hard look. It was as if time stood still... three people, sitting in silence, saying nothing but thinking everything. Robbie knew it was time to come clean. He took a deep breath, all choked up and eyes full of tears.

"I have something else to tell you."

He confessed in detail to the adventures of going to Brewster's and to Moe's, and about the close encounter with the *Sea Wolf* submarine and the Navy Police. He apologized for those as well.

While Mr. and Mrs. Morin heard his apologies, they were thinking more about the immediate danger Robbie had actually been in: incoming tide, high winds, strong current causing choppy waves, lightning, thunder and hail, and rocks all around, etc. Had *Dolittle* not stayed put on its anchor, it could have flipped over or been smashed on the rocks. Robbie could have been seriously hurt or drowned. Spruce Creek, though normally calm, in certain weather conditions can be a dangerous place. Also, it is very remote. There were no cars, houses or people on shore, and no way to signal for help. And since boaters hardly ever go to Spruce Creek, due to the low bridge clearance, no one would have known Robbie's whereabouts, except for perhaps a most unusual seagull. It was only by the grace of God that he was okay. It was

Robbie & George

like a miracle.

With a deep sigh of relief, Mr. and Mrs. Morin looked at each other, then at Robbie. They too had an admission to make as they had known all along about the "adventures" and kept a close watch on Robbie and George.

"Well, we knew about your trip to Brewster's," his mother said.

"You did?" Robbie asked.

"Your father suspected you were heading there for sea worms once you passed under the Navy Yard Bridge, so we called Mr. Brewster. He called back to let us know that you were fine and on your way home with your new friend George and a can of worms!"

Hmmmm, Robbie thought.

"Yeah and that day when you said you and George weren't hungry... not hungry, you?" his dad chuckled. "Your mother knew you were up to something, and Moe's was a sure bet."

"I called Mr. Moe and asked if he'd keep an eye out for you," said his mom. "He said that you had happily come and gone with your lunch and that you —"

"Still owe him 23 cents?" Robbie asked.

"Exactly!" she said. "I told him I thought you were good for it and besides, you smelled like Moes!"

Robbie sat quietly, his head spinning.

"Oh!" his dad said while cleaning his glasses on his shirt. "And the whole Navy Yard Police thing... it was

Caught in the Act

hard not to hear about it on the VHF radio. It's not too often you hear about a nine-year-old boy in a thirteen-foot whaler being stopped by the Federal Police!"

Robbie's jaw dropped, his eyes went wide as saucers...

"Were you going to say something, dear?" his mother asked.

He just shook his head instead of saying no.

What Robbie has not realized was that his parents had a network of friends on boats in the harbor and folks who lived in houses along the shore between Kittery and Portsmouth, including old Gus Alley who liked Robbie and always kept an eye on him. Everyone looked out for each other, including for their son. He was easy to spot with his orange lifejacket, light brown hair and big smile. Having a seagull on the bow of a little boat was a dead giveaway.

So, by either telephone or VHF radio, all were ready to help at a moment's notice if needed. His parents, like George, didn't miss a trick, except this once while they were away grocery shopping, when Robbie broke all three rules and ended up in a place so remote as to not be found.

After sitting there for a few minutes, with nothing more to say, Mr. Morin extended his hand and Robbie handed him *Dolittle's* bow line. Mr. Morin tied it to the stern cleat of the launch while Robbie pulled up *Dolittle's* anchor and coiled the lines. Mr. and Mrs. Morin towed Robbie and *Dolittle* back around the headland to the

Robbie & George

boatyard while George flew ahead. Robbie then cleaned up his muddy boots with the hose on the dock and gave *Dolittle* a much-needed scrubbing.

Robbie was waiting (and dreading) for his parents to revoke his privilege of using *Dolittle*. He knew it was coming. He climbed aboard *My Fair Lady*.

"Mom?" he said.

"Yes dear?"

"*Dolittle* is all cleaned up," he said, then paused and stared at the floor. With his voice quiet and hesitant he said, "I know the ground rules are in place for a reason, and today I broke them all. But will I still be allowed to use *Dolittle*?"

"Well Robbie, your father and I have discussed it. We very much appreciate your apology and for telling us the truth, something you should always do, especially to avoid situations like this. After all, we are all supposed to be best friends, aren't we? We are all in this together and we need to help each other out, don't we? While we forgive you for the things you have done and think you learned a valuable lesson today, we think you should take a break from using *Dolittle* for a while. We also feel you are ready to learn a few more skills." While Robbie was saddened by the news he perked up and wondered what kind of skills she was talking about.

Caught in the Act

Over the next few days, his parents revisited the situation several times, encouraging Robbie to think about what had happened, how it happened, what could have been done differently, and what will he do next time. They taught him how to read and understand the tide charts. Together, they listened to the marine weather forecast. They also introduced Robbie to the VHF radio and emphasized it was not a "walkie-talkie" type of toy. Robbie loved listening to the VHF radio, especially when the Coast Guard came on to report on boaters who may be in trouble! But he was not sure how to talk on it. At this point, his dad simply wanted him to listen. Talking on the VHF radio was for adults and carried a lot of responsibly.

Only a few days had passed, but it seemed like forever to Robbie. He was sitting on the deck of *My Fair Lady*, glumly staring down at *Dolittle*, with George sitting on the bow eager to get going. He was thinking regretfully about the situation he had gotten himself into when, like a miracle, his dad called him from the dock.

"Hey! I have an idea, why don't we fill up that gas tank, son? It looks like George wants to go fishing!"

"Really? Thanks Dad!" Robbie smiled. Barely

controlling his excitement, he ran to grab his life jacket. George was excited, too, as he started to waddle back and forth along the bow. While George had gained even more respect amongst the family, Robbie had gained a little, too.

Robbie started the engine while his father untied the bow and stern lines and tossed them in the boat. Robbie looked his father straight in the eyes and said, "I'm sorry, Dad."

His father replied, "I know you are... you're a good man, Charlie Brown." And off they went.

Summer's End

When summer came to an end, people became busy cleaning up their boats and packing their bags. It was time for the boat yard to haul and store the boats for the winter season. The Ellises had sailed back to the harbor after being away for the summer.

As they were settling *Sunday's Child* on their mooring, they heard, "Mr. and Mrs. Ellis! Mr. and Mrs. Ellliiiisssss!" It was Robbie shouting across the water and waving to get their attention. "I have so much to tell you!" he continued. He jumped into *Dolittle*, puttered over to *Sunday's Child*, and tied up and climbed aboard.

"Welcome aboard, Robbie! What's going on? How was your summer?" asked Mrs. Ellis.

Robbie told them of George, their adventures, Mrs. Labrie, the water taxi business, Spruce Creek, and how George had saved his life! "George has become my best friend!" announced Robbie proudly.

The Ellises were impressed with, but not surprised by,

Robbie & George

Robbie's summer with George. They knew, after all, that George was a most unusual seagull. At that exact moment, George landed with grace and precision on the side deck of *Sunday's Child*, right next to Robbie, where they had first met. He quickly shook his body, tilted his head from side to side, and wiggled his wings to put them back in place as if to say: "All right, what's next?"

They all laughed and laughed! George knew he could count on the Ellises for a slice of bread and so as not to disappoint, Mrs. Ellis went below and got a slice and handed it to Robbie who, piece by piece, fed it to George.

The Ellises told Robbie of the wonderful summer they had sailing to Bar Harbor, Maine, and how sad they were to see the season come to an end. They, too, had to pack up their bags and prepare their sailboat for winter storage. So Robbie gladly helped them gather their things and load them onto *Dolittle*. He made several trips back and forth to the dock for the Ellises and while they tried to tip him, he refused to accept any money.

"Chock it up to generosity!" said Robbie.

It was also time for the Morin's to move back inland to Manchester, New Hampshire, and for the school year to begin. Robbie was heartbroken. Heartbroken to leave the summer behind, but also to leave behind his best friend.

Summer's End

It was a long, painful Sunday packing up the car. George followed Robbie back and forth from the boat to the dock to the car as he and his parents carried duffel bags, sleeping bags, pillows, food, and all the rest.

George was wondering where they were going and what they were doing. They finally closed the windows, hatches and door to *My Fair Lady* and slowly and sadly walked to the car with their last load of bags. Mr. Morin started the car, put the windows down and Robbie and his mom reluctantly got in. Mr. Morin carefully backed out of the long, crushed-stone driveway.

Robbie couldn't see much because his eyes were full of tears, tears which ran down his face and fell on his shorts. His nose was running, his vision was blurred, and he kept holding his breath. George was walking alongside the car, trying to understand what was happening, possibly worrying about what he had done wrong. Mr. Morin backed into Dr. Lux's empty spot to turn the car around, shifted into forward gear, and away they went. Robbie was fighting back more tears and he heard his mother crying in the front seat. From the back seat he could see in the rear-view mirror that his father was crying too and wiping away tears from his eyes. Just the thought of packing everything up and leaving their summer life behind was hard enough, but to leave George there all alone was a different matter. Robbie's mom gave each of them some Kleenex.

As they drove across the Memorial Bridge into Portsmouth, there was only one seagull circling over the span of the bridge, flying back and forth, following the car. It was George. Robbie waved his arms out the window.

"GOOD-BYE GEORGE," he wailed, with a lump in his throat. Once clear of the bridge, George circled around the moving car three times, and then headed towards the Back Channel, back towards Dion's, probably guessing they would be coming back. Robbie was so confused and so tired of thinking about it all that he leaned over onto the pillow and bags of dirty clothes in the back seat and fell fast asleep.

Summer's End

The Painting

During the beginning of the busy school year, Robbie's thoughts of George began to dwindle, but only slightly. He often thought of the promised painting by Mrs. Rose Labrie. In addition to going to school and doing homework, Robbie kept busy delivering newspapers and did as many chores as he could to save up money toward buying the hoped-for painting.

In December, a letter came from Mrs. Labrie, telling Robbie that she had finished the painting. "*Word has reached me,*" she wrote, "*that you have been working very hard and saving your money diligently. It is time to stop your hard work and come to pick up the painting here at my home in Portsmouth. I have invited your parents to bring you next Saturday at 2:00 pm.*"

Oh Wow! thought Robbie. She really *had* painted the painting of him and George! Robbie started dreaming of the painting, like a colorful postcard, sitting on the little nightstand next to his bed. Or maybe he'd let his parents display it on the fireplace mantel or Scotch Tape it to the

The Painting

refrigerator door so they could all see it every day.

When Robbie and his parents arrived at Mrs. Labrie's house on that Saturday afternoon, they noticed they were not the only ones there. The snow-covered driveway, lawn, and street were full of cars and vans, and even a pickup truck. Mr. Morin figured that Mrs. Labrie must be having a holiday art sale, and because she was famous in the area, many people purchased her artwork as gifts. Robbie was not thinking about that. He wanted to see the painting and give Mrs. Labrie the purple velvet pouch of his hard-earned money. When she came out the front door, he ran up to her and gave her a big hug, taking care not to crush the red rose pinned to her dress.

"Hello, Mrs. Labrie!" he shouted.

"Hi Robbie! You've gotten much taller since the summer! Have you been working hard and saving your money?"

He handed her the velvet pouch and said proudly, "Yes I have! Here is all of my savings… 42 dollars and 33 cents!"

"That's wonderful." She smiled warmly. She explained that she wanted the painting to be a surprise and was going to blindfold Robbie, walk him into the house, then remove the blindfold. She knew Robbie would recognize the painting instantly, but she wanted him to find it on his own. She tied the blindfold around his head to cover his eyes, held his hand, and walked him inside.

"Okay, ready? 1, 2, 3!" and she removed his blindfold.

Robbie & George

There were so many paintings! And there were also television crews and reporters from magazines, newspapers and the local radio station, too! But he wasn't thinking about them. Robbie wandered through the rooms; there were paintings everywhere. He was looking for a small post-card sized painting of himself, George, and *Dolittle*, but he could not find it. He looked and looked.

Mrs. Labrie seemed a little disappointed that he could not find the painting. She walked Robbie back toward the front door in front of flashing cameras, back to the entrance where they had started.

"Look again!" she said as she turned him around. And there it was, right in front of him on an easel! It was the width of Robbie's arms stretched out wide, and so much bigger than what he and his parents were expecting. There were many shades of blue and white, purple and yellow, displaying little *Dolittle*, Robbie in his red jacket, and George standing proudly on the bow. It even had a gold name plaque on it that read *Robbie and George at Sea by Rose Labrie*. Robbie's eyes opened wide, and his mouth made a round O. He was speechless.

Mr. and Mrs. Morin suddenly understood what all the commotion was about with the cars, the lights, and cameras. There was no art show, no holiday sale. It was all about Robbie and George. Rose Labrie had found the friendship of boy and bird fascinating and shared this story with the media, who thought many viewers and

The Painting

readers would also be interested. Robbie and his parents were overwhelmed with surprise and pride.

Robbie & George

"Oh Mrs. Labrie! I just can't believe it! I was looking for something this size (Robbie made a square with his hands) but this is amazing!" Robbie had tears in his eyes. He gave Mrs. Labrie the biggest hug he had ever given anyone.

On the drive home that afternoon, all Robbie could talk about was hanging the painting on his bedroom wall. All his mom could talk about was what a great opportunity it was for Robbie to thoroughly clean his entire bedroom. This included going through his bureau, closet, and desk drawers, taking down posters, washing the floors, and painting the walls before the painting could be mounted on his bedroom wall. To Robbie that seemed like overkill, but after a couple of days of much needed cleaning and sprucing up, there was a wall in his newly freshened bedroom dedicated to *Robbie and George at Sea by Rose Labrie*.

Each day during the winter Robbie looked at the painting and thought about George, especially during snowstorms, high winds and freezing temperatures. Where was that most unusual seagull, and how was he doing? Were the other seagulls picking on him? Robbie hoped he was alright. Of course, seagulls are self-sufficient, even weatherproof, but Robbie didn't know how George would fare during the harsh New England winter. Robbie hoped George felt the same way about missing him. How fine it would be, he wished, if he could write to George, and George could write back. The

The Painting

painting warmed his heart and reminded him of the adventures the two of them had during the summer. Daydreaming of those things made the school year go by quickly. Robbie had gained so much confidence in himself and enjoyed telling the kids at school of his adventures with George.

Spring at Last

Winter turned into spring and, when the school year came to an end, Robbie and his parents packed up the car to go back to live aboard *My Fair Lady* for the summer. Robbie couldn't wait to get back on the boat, get *Dolittle* in the water, look for George, and go fishing again.

The family left their house in Manchester and drove the long 55 miles to Kittery. This time, Robbie was wide awake and practically bouncing up and down on the back seat. He could hardly contain his excitement! His legs were shaking, his heart was pumping, and he was full of anticipation about the summer ahead. As soon as the car reached their assigned parking spot, Robbie grabbed his backpack, jumped out of the car, and started to run barefoot down the crushed-stone parking area towards the dock without a care about getting stones between his toes.

"AHEM!" his mother said loudly. "Hold on, where do you think you are going?"

Spring at Last

Robbie stopped... "Ooops!"

One of the other family rules was no one goes empty-handed between the car and the boat. There were always things that needed to be carried in both directions. So he ran back to the car, picked up his pillow and sleeping bag, and turned toward *My Fair Lady* once again.

At the top of the ramp, just above the docks, he stopped and dropped everything. He stood on his tiptoes, craning his neck. He held his right arm in the air to block the sun's rays and squinted his eyes to look across the harbor. He looked and looked.

And there he was, standing on his familiar rock, all alone.

Robbie cupped his hands around his mouth and yelled out "GEEOOOORGE!" at the top of his lungs. His parents had caught up to Robbie, their arms loaded with grocery sacks and duffel bags.

"Shush!" they said in unison, knowing that everyone in the harbor could hear their son making a racket. Then they too dropped their bags to the ground in total disbelief.

All three of them watched as George spread his wings and leapt off his rock. He flew several big, graceful circles high overhead, surveying the situation, and then dropped down and landed precisely next to Robbie. Mr. and Mrs. Morin were stunned and speechless. As the four of them stood there, his parents looked from Robbie to George to each other, and back to Robbie and George again. They could not believe a mere seagull could remember one specific boy after many months apart. But of course, George was a most unusual seagull.

George quickly shook his body, tilted his head from side to side, wiggled his wings as if to put them back in place and looked at the three of them as if to say: "All right, where have you been all this time? And what's next?"

And another summer of adventures began…

Author's Note

This book is based on a true story about being a kid and about having best friends. Best friends don't necessarily have to be another boy or a girl, they don't have to look the same, be the same color or even have the same beliefs. Best friends can be dogs, cats, imaginary friends, and parents too... mine just happened to be a seagull.

As of this writing in 2022, "Robbie and George at Sea" by Rose Labrie still hangs proudly in the author's bedroom, and Dolittle can often be seen plying the waters in and around Sandusky Bay in Ohio.

Robbie, summer 1974

Bob, Betsy & Robbie Morin, July 4 th, 1964
(Robbie was born in September)

My Fair Lady at sea with Robbie at the helm standing on his Father's milk crate

My Fair Lady tied in her slip at Dion's Yacht Yard

Rose Labrie in her white dress and red roses

Her painting of Robbie and George at Sea

Robbie and "George" at Sea, 1974
Oil on canvas
Collection of Robert Morin

At a reception in Portsmouth many years ago, a little blond boy, about eight years old, came running over to me. He was looking at my dress (a white colonial gown with ruffles and a big red rose) and said that it was very nice.

He was also full of wonderment about the paintings and wanted to know if I had painted them. When I told him I had, he asked if I could paint him a picture. Of course, when I told him the price of the paintings, he said he couldn't possibly buy one. I asked him why he wanted a painting so much and he told me his best friend was a seagull named George, who was now gone, and he wanted a painting of him. He stayed with me while his mother went to do some errands, and he exclaimed over all the pictures. When the crowd finally thinned out and we were able to talk, we made an agreement: it was July and he agreed to work and save all his money until Christmas and whatever he saved by then would be the price of the painting. I decided to do more than just a little painting of a seagull, but didn't tell him that. I wrote to him a week before Christmas and told him that whatever he had saved by them would be enough, that he should enjoy the Christmas preparations and stop working. When he came to my house with his parents, we put a blindfold on him and led him into the dining room where I had hung the painting. We took the blindfold off, and the poor kid couldn't see the painting because he was looking for a little painting of a seagull. He had brought me the money in a big velvet pouch, which I will always keep; it was loaded with money, about $46, much of it in dollar bills and about $25 in silver. He was so happy and so was I. It was really a very moving experience for me.

—Rose Labrie, 1983

Robbie's order at Moe's

George on the lookout for fish

Whaleback Lighthouse: "Whoooomp, Whoooomp!"

Acknowledgements

Thanks to Tom Holbrook for believing in and accepting my manuscript and for managing the publishing project from start to finish. Thanks for not giving up on me and with the best of intentions, trying to make me a writer! You helped make the story much better.

A special thanks to Larry Daley for bringing his positive energy, enthusiasm, creativity, ideas, imagination, and professional experience to a 'blank canvas' in creating the superb illustrations that amazingly brought this story to life! Since the outset, he immersed himself in this project and he never looked back. He did what I never dreamed could be done... an incredible accomplishment! I'm forever grateful for his sincere interest, involvement, and significant contributions.

I'd also like to thank the many people who, over the years, have touched or been touched by this story whether for a few minutes or a few decades. The story has been shared with and well received by folks both in the states and abroad and it's been their retelling of the story that keeps it alive, fun, and truly never-ending. Thanks for your love, laughter, and support. It's been a blessing to have you all in my life!

Rob Morin grew up in New Hampshire and spent a few summers of his childhood living on a boat with his parents in Maine. Those years and this story set the stage for the amazing decades that followed. Much of his life has been spent power boating, sailing and traveling to other countries by sea. No matter where he's been or goes, his friend George is always with him. In part, this story is about how parents and best friends can have a huge impact on a child of an impressionable age. Today, he shares the story of Robbie and George as his first book.

Larry Daley spent many years as a creative director for DC Comics and Warner Bros. Studios, helping to develop characters like BATMAN and SUPERMAN for feature films. He grew up fishing the local streams of New Hampshire until his family finally convinced dad to buy a fish-n-ski boat and ditch the canoe! Whether it was fishing for bass in Lake Winnisquam or riding the ocean spray out to the Isles of Shoals, their little boat brought out the best in their family and inspired Larry to draw cartoons of their crazy boating adventures. Today, he spends his time illustrating while enjoying life on the New Hampshire seacoast with his family. To see a collection of Larry's illustrations, please visit www.larrydaley.com

Made in United States
North Haven, CT
30 September 2022